Twayne's Theatrical Arts Series

Warren French
EDITOR

Grigori Kozintsev

Grigori Kozintsev at the time of the filming of *King Lear*.

Grigori Kozintsev

BARBARA LEAMING

Hunter College
City University of New York

BOSTON

Twayne Publishers

1980

Grigori Kozintsev

Published in 1980 by Twayne Publishers,
A Division of G.K. Hall & Co.

Copyright © 1980 by G. K. Hall & Co.

Printed on permanent/durable acid-free paper and bound
in the United States of America

Library of Congress Cataloging in Publication Data

Leaming, Barbara.
  Grigori Kozintsev.

  (Twayne's theatrical arts series)
  Bibliography: p. 145
  Filmography: p. 147
  Includes index.
  1. Kozintsev, Grigori Mikhailovich.
PN1998.A3K686   791.43'0233'0924   80-14128
ISBN 0-8057-9276-7

Contents

About the Author

BARBARA LEAMING is an assistant professor in the Department of Theatre and Cinema at Hunter College of the City University of New York. She holds a Ph.D. and an M.A. in cinema studies from New York University, as well as an M.A. in Russian Area Studies from Hunter College and a B.A. in Russian Civilization from Smith College. Professor Leaming has published articles in journals and anthologies in the United States, Canada, and Europe.

Editor's Foreword

OF THE FILMMAKERS celebrated in this series, Grigori Kozintsev is one of those whom I—and I suspect most Americans—know least well, because of the poor distribution of his films in the United States. This situation is especially unfortunate because Kozintsev is one of the most remarkable figures in film history. He is one of those rare Soviet filmmakers who produced major work in all periods of Soviet film history to the present, from the experimental 1920s, through the oppressive years of Stalinist Socialist Realism, to the "thaw" in Russian cultural life following the demise of Stalin. During this last period, in fact, an aging Kozintsev created his three greatest films in adaptations of three of the most profound classics of the Renaissance West—*Don Quixote, Hamlet, King Lear.*

Like Luis Buñuel—who, though finally more prolific, has an intriguingly parallel achievement—Kozintsev is one of the most remarkable examples in cultural history of the difficult art of survival. The incomprehensible thing about his genius is how he was able to maintain his resiliency, keep his hopes alive and his energies harnessed through two frustrating decades to reach his peak, also like Buñuel, at an age when many once promising talents (like Orson Welles's) have been dissipated.

His astonishing energy is apparent from the frantic action of his early agit-prop films that left American reviewers of the 1920s exhausted and bewildered. Without this energy and an unflagging talent, he could never have achieved what he did; yet while these characteristics distinguish him from most other filmmakers, what truly sets him apart is his confidence in his vision that enabled him to keep his dream alive in the face of demoralizing frustrations. Small wonder that Kozintsev identified strongly with Don Quixote! He was himself a Quixote of a dehumanizing age.

When Barbara Leaming proposed this first extensive study in English of Kozintsev's work, I was particularly excited because one of the special aims of this series is to introduce Americans to important auteurs like Kozintsev and Abel Grance and Peter Watkins, who have not received sufficient attention in this country. Certainly if anyone merits the controversial designation *auteur*, it is Kozintsev, who, with his long-time collaborator Leonid Trauberg and later alone, wrote most of his own scripts and worked out his own adaptations of classic works from other genres. The extent to which his vision, when freed from bureaucratic restraints, has shaped his films is shown not just by the films themselves, but also by the two remarkable "diaries" upon which Professor Leaming draws extensively in explaining Kozintsev's final major works—*Shakespare: Time and Conscience* and *King Lear: The Space of Tragedy.* The happy preservation of these two unique self-revelations provides an invaluable introduction into the mind of a man who "thinks cinematically" and perceives film as a great autonomous art.

Professor Leaming's book is, wisely, precisely an *introduction* to Kozintsev. So complicated are his major works and personal history and so little is his achievement understood in the United States that the present book concentrates upon providing a detailed guide only to that part of Kozintsev's work that is readily available for showing and study in this country. As Professor Leaming intends, this book, which she aptly describes as an "analysis of the politics of form," is only a beginning of the study of an important artist—already highly respected in his homeland—who will hopefully become subsequently the subject of wider international study from a diversity of viewpoints.

Fortunately, with the exception of *The New Babylon,* enough of this work is available to make a coherent study of the development of Kozintsev's artistry possible. From the early years the almost incredibly young Kozintsev and Trauberg's adaptation of Gogol's *The Cloak* and their *The Devil's Wheel* are available for comparison with the surrealist and other experimental productions of the French avant garde of the same period, as well as the strikingly anti-realistic films of the German Expressionists. While most of the Socialist Realist productions are not accessible for study at present, *The Youth of Maxim* may be compared with the "documentary realism" of artists like Pare Lorentz of the American 1930s and the later and vastly influential Italian Neo-realism to suggest how a personal vision and style can be manifested even in films primarily serving doctrinaire aims.

Best of all, however, Kozintsev's three major late films continue to be distributed in this country, so that we may learn why he enjoyed his greatest triumph in the United States on September 14, 1964, when his *Hamlet* was selected as the opening night attraction at the New York Film Festival and the creator himself appeared to receive the plaudits of the fashionable and knowledgeable crowd. The *New York Times*'s veteran reviewer Bosley Crowther headed his report the next day, "Regal Soviet 'Hamlet'" and observed that the film was "a fine achievement of pictorial plasticity and power" that "got the festival off to a spanking start." Regrettably, however, the film was not generally released in this country for another year and a half; and, although all three of these works showing Kozintsev's art in its full maturity have been highly praised by critics, Americans have been slow to come to terms with works that achieve uncommon profundity in visual, cinematic terms. Like great painters as well as other great filmmakers like Jean Renoir and again Buñuel, Kozintsev demands that audiences develop new "ways of seeing."

Hopefully Professor Leaming's illuminating analysis of the formal qualities of Kozintsev's work and his own explanation of his aims in his major films will lead to the development of ways of seeing that will make possible a broader appreciation of his accomplishment. Since Kozintsev remarkably overcame the obstacles of youthful inexperience, the technical limitations of a new and developing medium and bureaucratic controls to triumph in a visionary artist's struggle to fulfill himself, let us hope that he will also finally overcome—as once again Luis Buñuel has—the final and most frustrating obstacle that confronts the strikingly original artist—an audience unprepared to meet the demands that he makes of them.

W. F.

Preface

THE PAGES WHICH FOLLOW constitute the first English-language volume on the career of the Soviet filmmaker Grigori Kozintsev. Given the wide range and complexity of Kozintsev's cinematic *oeuvre,* these remarks will be only a first word. They have been undertaken in that spirit, as an attempt to initiate serious critical consideration of an artist who occupies the very first ranks of importance not just in the Soviet cinema, but in world cinema as well.

Many readers will no doubt come to this volume as a result of an encounter with the two great films of the director's maturity, the adaptations of William Shakespeare's *Hamlet* (1963) and *King Lear* (1969–71). For these readers, the present study should serve as an invitation to view Kozintsev's various other films, as well as to locate *Hamlet* and *King Lear* in relation to the structure of the director's *oeuvre* as a whole.

A scrutiny of this *oeuvre* permits a consideration of a number of fundamental aesthetic problems that pertain to the work of other filmmakers as well. For instance, the problem of the *avant-garde* and its complex relations to radical politics is central to this study of Kozintsev. Anyone concerned with the cinematic *avant-garde* that flourished in the Soviet Union in the 1920's, in conjunction with a more general *avant-garde* movement in the arts, will know of Kozintsev's legendary collaboration with Leonid Trauberg during that time. Indeed, there is today a great fascination with the role of the *avant-garde* in our century. As we move into a time that is often characterized as "post-modern," we are nevertheless still engaged in an attempt to assimilate as fully as possible the manifestations of the "modern" in the arts. In 1979, the mammoth exhibition called "Paris-Moscow" was mounted at the Georges Pompidou Center of Art and Culture in Paris. It served as an index of a current preoccupation with the *avant-garde* in general, and with the encounter of Soviet and Western examples in particular. The Soviet *avant-garde* of the 1920s was at once similar to and different from *avant-garde* movements in the West. Therefore, we look to its experience with special fascination, as the self gazes at its other.

In order to begin to consider Kozintsev's contribution to both Soviet and world cinema, it is essential to comprehend the precise historical context in which the young artist was formed. In October 1917 the Bolsheviks came to power in Russia. The final blow to centuries of tsarist oppression had been dealt. Russia's task at this point was to attempt to advance from incredible backwardness toward the horizon of a more promising future. It was immediately apparent that the shift in political power which had transpired had unleashed a tremendous reserve of creative energy in the society. The future was to belong to the workers and their allies. And, for many artists, there was a strong sense that the new society would need a new culture. Indeed, there were even indications of Lenin's own interest in the evolution of this new culture. A masterful politician, Lenin was quick to realize that, in a nation which was still 73 percent illiterate, the young medium of film could assume a powerful political role. In his fierce struggle to win the allegiance of Russia's enormous population, Lenin was soon to declare cinema to be "the most important art."

In 1919 Lenin nationalized the cinema, placing it under the direction of no less a personage than his wife. The issuance of the nationalization decree meant that all filmmakers became public employees. No longer was it purely a profit motive that was to direct the course of cinema. Instead, the cinema would operate to serve the needs of the victorious proletariat. It must be noted, however, that the film industry which Lenin nationalized was in a condition of great disorder. Many of the prerevolutionary filmmakers had fled after the October Revolution, often taking with them precious equipment and raw stock, which could not immediately be replaced from native sources, since they were not then manufactured in Russia.

This chaotic state of affairs would have significant implications for talented youngsters like Kozintsev. One of the effects of the flight of experienced filmmakers was that the cinema became, in essence, an open field. It mattered little how young a director, actor, or cameraman might be. There was plenty of room for the enterprising young person, even though he may have lacked experience. Remarkably, at the age of nineteen, when he codirected with Trauberg a first feature film, Kozintsev already had several years of theatrical experience behind him! Indeed, the youth of these filmmakers who revolutionized their art form in those exciting years is a crucial factor for a comprehension of the development of Soviet *avant-garde* cinema.

Next, a study of Kozintsev's cinematic *oeuvre* must take us through the painful transition to Socialist Realism in the 1930s. The imposition of the Socialist Realist aesthetic in the 1930s involved a dismantling of the *avant-garde* of the previous decade. The relevant scene to be examined here is the First Congress of Soviet Writers, which was held in Moscow in 1934. The moment in intellectual history it marks is relevant not simply to literature, but to the other arts as well. There, Andrei Zhdanov, secretary of the Central Committee of the Communist party, presented the address, which may be located as the official statement of the Socialist Realist aesthetic. At that same gathering, Karl Radek delivered another address that is particularly relevant to our concerns here. In it, Radek subjected the modernist literary production of James Joyce to a harsh critique. Joyce functioned, in essence, as a synecdoche for modernism and its various manifestations in the arts. In attacking Joyce, Radek implicated the entire modern art movement. Indeed, it might be said that Socialist Realism involved a retrieval of aspects of nineteenth-century "Realist" aesthetics.

A consideration of Soviet Socialist Realism as it evolved in the 1930s engages us in the problems posed by the politics of form. Moreover, it suggests the more general problem of "Realism," an issue of central concern in today's aesthetics. As a filmmaker who operated successfully in both the *avant-garde* cinema of the 1920s and the Socialist Realist cinema which emerged in the 1930s, Kozintsev makes possible a comparative study of the two aesthetic approaches. Socialist Realism is, of course, associated with triumphant Stalinism. What, then, of the Soviet cinema after Stalin's death? Kozintsev's films are instructive in this regard, as well. The director's final works permit a glimpse of the post-Stalinist cinema at its absolute best and must be comprehended within that precise context. With them, Kozintsev reassumed a vanguard position in the Soviet cinema, as in the world cinema.

In order to comprehend the structure of Kozintsev's *oeuvre* as a whole, the present study will consider his films not in isolation, but intertextually, that is, in relation to each other, and to the text of world cinema in general. In addition, the theoretical writings of Kozintsev are frequently consulted—especially in the final chapters—not in order to discern the director's intentions, but, rather, to comprehend the complex intertextual relations between his visual and verbal enterprises. Since not all of Kozintsev's films are available for rental in the United States, greatest attention is generally paid to those films which the reader will be able to consider firsthand. Again, it is hoped that the present study will serve to direct further attention—both critical and general—to the work of this superb Soviet director.

The author wishes to acknowledge the early support of the project by Warren French, and the kind help of Ted Perry and Charles Silver of the Museum of Modern Art in New York, as well as Jacques Ledoux and the staff of the Royal Film Archive of Belgium. In addition, Laurie Goldbas, Diana Torbarina and Ronald R. Erickson (Media Interface) provided invaluable assistance in the course of this project.

This volume is dedicated to the author's aunt, Virginia N. Brown.

Chronology

1905 Grigori Kozintsev is born in Kiev on March 22.

1917 The Bolsheviks seize power.

1919 Kozintsev goes to Petrograd.

1922 Manifestos on Eccentrism are published. The Factory of the Eccentric Actor is opened. FEKS stages its first production, a version of Gogol's "Marriage," which they call "A Gag in Three Acts: The Electrification of Gogol."

1924 The first FEKS film, *The Adventures of Octyabrina.*

1925 *Mishka Against Yudenitch.*

1926 *The Devil's Wheel; The Cloak.*

1927 *Little Brother; S.V.D. or The Club of the Big Deed;* Vladimir Mayakovsky writes a script for FEKS that will not be realized.

1928 The Kabuki theater visits Russia, and Kozintsev attends regularly.

1929 *The New Babylon.*

1931 *Alone,* a film which begins to mark a break with the *avant-garde* style of the 1920s.

1932 Friedrich Ermler's *Counterplan* initiates the Socialist Realist cinema.

1934 First Congress of Soviet Writers in Moscow. The aesthetic of Socialist Realism is announced. Sergei and Georgy Vasiliev's *Chapayev,* the model Socialist Realist film.

1935 *The Youth of Maxim.*

1937 *The Return of Maxim.*

1939 *The Vyborg Side.*

1939– Kozintsev and Trauberg prepare to make a film on the
1940 life of Karl Marx. The project is never realized.

1941 The Maxim Trilogy wins the Stalin Prize.

1941   *Film Notes on Battles No. 1 and 2.* Kozintsev stages *King Lear.*

1945   *Simple People* (not released until 1956).

1946   The Central Committee of the Communist party issues a resolution entitled "On the Moving Picture *Great Life.*" Kozintsev and Trauberg's *Simple People* is attacked, along with other films. The collaboration of Kozintsev and Trauberg draws to an end.

1947   Kozintsev makes his debut as a solo film director with *Pirogov.* Trauberg writes the screenplay for *Life in the Citadel,* directed by Herbert Rappoport.

1949   Campaign against the "cosmopolitans," in which Trauberg is attacked directly; and Kozintsev, implicitly.

1953   Stalin dies.

1953-   Kozintsev stages *Hamlet.*
1954

1956   Khrushchev makes his "Secret Speech" at the Twentieth Congress of the Soviet Communist party, in which Stalin is attacked. *Simple People* released.

1957   *Don Quixote.*

1963   *Hamlet.*

1965   Kozintsev wins the Lenin Prize for *Hamlet.*

1969-   *King Lear.*
1971

1973   Kozintsev dies in Leningrad on May 11.

ЭКСЦЕН ТРИЗМ

ГРИГОРИЙ КОЗИНЦЕВ
ГЕОРГИЙ КРЫЖИЦКИЙ
ЛЕОНИД ТРАУБЕРГ
СЕРГЕЙ ЮТКЕВИЧ

1922

ЭКСЦЕНТРОПОЛИС
(БЫВШ. ПЕТРОГРАД)

1

Life and Times

GRIGORI KOZINTSEV was still a schoolboy when the Russian Revolution broke out. In more stable times, perhaps, it would have been strange indeed for such a young man to play an active role in the artistic life of his day. But the political turmoil of the Revolution engendered in its wake an absolutely overwhelming sweep of artistic activity and innovation. So furious and pervasive was the artistic enterprise accompanying the first years of the Revolution that even a youngster like Kozintsev might find himself engaged in it. Indeed, the entire future course of Kozintsev's rich artistic life was influenced by the Revolution and his response to it.

Kozintsev was to become one of the most critically and theoretically interesting figures in the history of Soviet film, for he was perhaps unique in having made a vital contribution to each of its major periods before his death. Thus, to study the films of Kozintsev is also to trace through a paradigm the major developments of the cinema in which he operated. In collaboration with his partner of half a lifetime, Leonid Trauberg, Kozintsev began to make films during the *avant-garde* period of the 1920s, the so-called "Golden Age" of the Soviet cinema. Kozintsev and Trauberg's work in these legendary early years represented significant steps in the elaboration of a new language for the cinema. With the consolidation of Stalinism in the 1930s, the cinema faced a joint crisis: the coming of sound and the imposition of an official and obligatory new aesthetic, Socialist Realism. The world cinema, of course, faced the aesthetic problems posed by the imposition of sound, but the Soviet cinema encountered the additional problems of Socialist Realism. This period witnessed the tragic destruction of the

17

The first page of the 1922 Manifesto of Eccentrism

careers of a number of the great Soviet artists of the 1920s. Yet somehow, during this difficult period of political and aesthetic crisis, Kozintsev and Trauberg were able to make what may be the most aesthetically satisfying film in the Socialist Realist cinema, *The Youth of Maxim* (1937).

They were both to suffer enormously, however, before long, for they were not immune to the tragedy of the Soviet cinema during the years of triumphant Stalinism. But after the death of Stalin, Kozintsev's career was to provide us with the opportunity to witness a truly stunning resurgence. In the post-Stalin years, Kozintsev was one of the first filmmakers to challenge the virtual ossification of the once great Soviet cinema. His last films, superb adaptations of great literary classics by Cervantes and Shakespeare, were to indicate that, until the very end of his life, Kozintsev had remained an artist of the Revolution. Both his youthful drive and his revolutionary spirit are intrinsic to the portrait of Kozintsev which emerges in the pages that follow.

Kozintsev was born in Kiev, the capital city of the Ukraine, on March 22, 1905. Kozintsev has remarked upon the very strange character of his education during that period of time spent in the Kiev gymnasium. The young schoolboy's classroom was no innocent playground marked off from the world of experience. After all, these were the early years of the Revolution, during which classroom activity was frequently punctuated by sounds of violence and destruction. Indeed, within the classroom, Kozintsev encountered rather startling experiential juxtapositions characteristic of violent upheaval: "Our teacher described the flora and fauna of Africa, explained the conjugation of Latin verbs," he recalls, "and meanwhile machine-guns chattered in the suburbs."[1] In this remarkable sentence—a record of childhood experience—we detect that principle of montage, founded upon collision, which would play so important a role in the development of Soviet *avant-garde* art. Such experiential juxtapositions as Kozintsev records here might be taken to adumbrate a later taste for aesthetic juxtaposition, as evinced in his *avant-garde* efforts. Radical juxtaposition would become a fundamental tactic of Kozintsev's early work.

Thus the sights and sounds of the chaotic period of the Revolution made an indelible impression upon the young Kozintsev. In later years, images of the time's violence and destruction would remain etched in his mind. He would recall auditory impressions, such as different guns, identifiable by their distinctive sounds, as well as visual impressions, such as the blood which gushed from a man's face. There is a sense in which these recollections might be described as cinematic in their attention to the sharpness of visual and auditory detail. Kozintsev has noted that he was later to appropriate such images of the past in his film *The Vyborg Side* (1939).

When Schors's troops marched into Kiev, they brought the city into a course of events which would change not merely the life of this young student, but that of an entire land. The world as Kozintsev had known it was changing rapidly from minute to minute, right within the space of his own city. It was not long before Kozintsev managed to find his way into the midst of the artistic activity in Kiev. Indeed, there was now a great upsurge of creative activity, which accompanied the coming of the Revolution. Even before he left school, Kozintsev enrolled in an art class under the direction of the great modernist painter Alexandra Exter.

Kozintsev's experience in Exter's class reveals something of the lively character of his thought, even so early in his life. Faced by the task of representing still lifes, Kozintsev turned elsewhere: "other images obsessed my mind: I heard the brass of a military band; the characters of well-loved books came and went before my eyes, violently, strangely lit as if by footlights; sparks flew from clashing swords; I saw the gleaming green eyes of the wizard from Gogol's *The Frightful Vengeance,* and spurring their horses, the Three Musketeers, leaping ravines."[2] These lines chronicle a poetics of reverie. Movement in its many forms displaces stasis, associated with the still-life project. Examined carefully, this reverie suggests what were to be Kozintsev's true artistic concerns during his *avant-garde* period. The montage of images looks ahead to the tactic of collision and juxtaposition which would so preoccupy him. In the reverie which Kozintsev records here, juxtaposition—even if within the form of fragmentary daydreams—displaces the task of representation, as it would in the artist's later aesthetic enterprise. Now, instead of limiting himself to those still lifes which were assigned in class, Kozintsev chose to work in such peripheral areas as caricature and parody. The radical, irreverent sensibility that would become his trademark as a director was already developing.

It was with the assistance of friends from Exter's painting class that the young Kozintsev was invited to work on the decoration of an agit-train. One of the characteristic Soviet phenomena of the time, the agit-train was a propaganda vehicle which moved through the country as it spread the latest word of the Revolution. It is important to note, then, that Kozintsev's initial activity in the world of art was one which firmly proclaimed the essential relationship between aesthetics and politics. For the rest of his career, a conception of the politics of form was to be, in deepened and more articulated manner, a basic tenet of Kozintsev's approach.

Sergei Yutkevitch

Once his participation in the decoration of the agit-train was completed, Kozintsev was allowed to travel with it as part of the agit-crew. It was at this time that the youngster worked on his first theatrical production, an agit-sketch, which was a brief political performance done on the train. Returning to Kiev after this initial experience, Kozintsev went to work at the Lenin Theater, previously known as the Solutzovsky Theater. His task there was to assist one of the scenery painters, Isaac Rabinovitch. In a burst of daring, Kozintsev showed his sketches to one of the directors of the theater, Konstantin Mardjanov. As a result, Kozintsev found himself called upon to work with another young painter on the designs for a play. This other youngster was Sergei Yutkevitch, who would one day become another of the renowned Soviet film directors. Kozintsev has vividly recalled his first impression of Yutkevitch with his "pointed nose" and twirling cane.[3] Specifically, the task before these two talented young fellows was to conceive the decor for an operetta, *La Mascotte*. Their collaboration was mutually satisfying and led to further partnership.

Together, Kozintsev and Yutkevitch secured the necessary permission to found a theater of their own in an abandoned cabaret located in a dismal cellar. The cabaret which they now appropriated for their purposes had been called Jimmy-le-Borgne; soon it would become a center for innovative theatrical practice. Like so many artists in this time and place, Kozintsev and Yutkevitch were fascinated by the great Russian Futurist

poet Vladimir Mayakovsky. Indeed, Mayakovsky became something of a hero for them. So it is hardly surprising that the first
production which they mounted was a performance of
Mayakovsky's play *Vladimir Mayakovsky.*

Kozintsev has recalled that neither he nor his youthful friends
of the period really understood much of what Mayakovsky was
doing in his work: "But the race of the rhythms and images, the
eruptive power of every line welled in our hearts. Pleasure and
joy caught our breaths: the vision of a new and marvelous world
filled us with ecstasy."[4] Like the Revolution itself, perhaps,
Mayakovsky was welcomed intuitively at first. His was the voice
of change, the sign of the future. Kozintsev immersed himself in
the pleasure of the text, even if he was not quite certain as to
what it was all about. What was the youngsters' practical
approach to this text, which they thought something of "an
indecipherable mystery"?[5] Following a shrewd hint provided by
the ever-helpful and sympathetic Mardjanov, Kozintsev and
Yutkevitch turned to their own intense interest in the circus.
Perhaps the circus, then, might provide a means for mounting
their production. What tactics were to be appropriated from the
circus world? Specifically, the lessons of the clown were thought
to offer possible solutions to the aesthetic problems that now
confronted them. Kozintsev set forth to compose a production
deeply influenced by two clowns whose work had interested him
in the past, Fernandez and Frico. Indeed, Kozintsev had viewed
their antics with great delight at the circus which he frequented.
The clowns, in turn, were delighted by the interest of the young
artists, and attempted to help them in various ways, such as
lending their costumes for the production. It might be said that
this production marked an intersection between art and popular
form which would prove so important to Kozintsev in the future.

After their creative staging of the Mayakovsky play, Kozintsev
and his friends went on to do puppet theater. A production of a
Pushkin text, *The Priest and His Servant Balda,* played in various
spots. Still later, they staged a play in a public square. Kozintsev
has recalled having missed its opening due to a bout with
typhoid. The evidence suggests, then, that Kozintsev's early
collaboration with Yutkevitch was an exuberant one indeed, in
which both young men tested various innovative artistic
possibilities.

Eventually, the Union of Art Workers of Kiev decided to send Kozintsev to Petrograd—as Leningrad was then called—for further training. In Petrograd he once again encountered Mardjanov, who now invited him to join his theatrical group. Never one inclined to do a single thing at a time, Kozintsev also continued his studies as a painter by enrolling at the Academy of Fine Arts, where Nathan Altmann, among others, taught. The period of time spent in this artistic milieu must have been exciting indeed! There was a strong sense in the air that this was a special time and place. Kozintsev characterizes the spirit of the age by noting that "there was no doubt at all that this moment marked the coming of a new era, the era of art."[6] But what would be the precise nature of this new era? As we might expect, literary and artistic debates exploded in this period, and the young Kozintsev was dazzled by their force. The art to be developed now, Kozintsev has noted, "had to be as bold as the workers' power itself, as pitiless toward the past as the Revolution."[7]

Leonid Trauberg

It was during this crucial early period in Petrograd that Kozintsev first encountered another young man who would play a decisive role in his life and career. Also newly arrived in Petrograd, Leonid Trauberg was three years Kozintsev's senior. Kozintsev and Trauberg quickly became friends, and thus established a partnership which was to endure for the next three decades. Indeed, their collaboration was one of the truly great artistic partnerships in the history of world cinema. During this initial phase, Kozintsev and Trauberg involved themselves with a lively group of friends which included Yutkevitch, as well as Alexei Kapler—with whom Kozintsev had already worked in Kiev—and Georgii Kryjitzki. In 1921, the friends founded the seminal theatrical enterprise known as The Factory of the Eccentric Actor (FEKS). That such very young men should be able to launch artistic activity of such significance is truly astounding! Indeed, another participant in the early days of FEKS, Sergei Gerassimov, has remarked that the youngsters looked upon people of twenty as " 'masters'. . . 'old ones,' rich in experience, belonging almost to another generation."[8]

The first FEKS play was a highly eccentric production of Gogol's *Marriage*. As we shall see, the theatrical notions of FEKS were very much of the times. Eventually, under the direction of Kozintsev and Trauberg, FEKS shifted from theater to cinema. The partners managed to get a scenario they had written accepted by Sevzapkino, or North-Western Cinema. When they first arrived, Sevzapkino possessed only a single, small studio, but that was enough for the inventive Kozintsev and Trauberg! In 1924, then, Kozintsev and Trauberg directed their first film, *The Adventures of Oktyabrina*. This film launched their long-term cinematic partnership. A second film followed in 1925, *Mishka Against Yudenitch*. Later, in 1926, the young directors achieved what is generally thought to be their first real success in the medium with *The Devil's Wheel*. Also in 1926, they presented *The Cloak*, a film based on literary material from Gogol. In 1927, Kozintsev and Trauberg once again launched two films, *Little Brother* and *S.V.D., or The Club of the Big Deed*. The final silent film directed by Kozintsev and Trauberg was *The New Babylon* in 1929.

Kozintsev and Trauberg's first effort in the sound cinema was *Alone* in 1931, a film which marks a bridge to Socialist Realism. And then, when the careers of so many other filmmakers were floundering as a result of the new demands of the Socialist Realist aesthetic, Kozintsev and Trauberg released the first film in their trilogy about Maxim, *The Youth of Maxim*, in 1934. The second part of the trilogy followed in 1937, *The Return of Maxim;* and the final part, The Vyborg Side, in 1939. By the time Kozintsev and Trauberg made *The Vyborg Side*, the demands of Socialist Realism had begun to have a powerfully inhibiting effect on their own work as well. The trilogy, then, is largely remembered for the remarkable *The Youth of Maxim*, a great achievement in the generally dismal context of the Socialist Realist cinema.

In 1941, during the war, Kozintsev and Trauberg made *Film Notes on Battles No. 1 and 2*. Next, the film *Simple People*, completed in 1945, was the last collaborative effort of Kozintsev and Trauberg. The film was subjected to a searing political attack and was only released in the period of liberalization after the death of Stalin. *Simple People*, then, marks the conclusion of one of the cinema's greatest partnerships.

The Solo Director

In 1947, then, Kozintsev and Trauberg were operating on their own. Trauberg emerged as a screen-writer, while Kozintsev continued to direct. Antonin and Mira Liehm have commented that although "they each came out with a new film in 1947, . . . the spark was gone."[9] Trauberg's screenplay for the film *Life in the Citadel* focuses on the effects of war and political conflict upon a family. Trauberg based his screenplay on an Estonian text by August Jakobson. The film was directed by Herbert Rappoport. Kozintsev's first effort as a solo director was the film *Pirogov,* also in 1947. The work is a cinematic biography of a surgeon of the previous century. Next, in 1951, Kozintsev made a film entitled *Belinsky,* which found its inspiration in the well-known Radical Critic.

But it was to be Kozintsev's next three films—tragically the last of his career—which would assure him a firm position in the history of world cinema. In succession, the director managed to create three truly great films, *Don Quixote, Hamlet,* and *King Lear.* Together, they form a remarkable conclusion to the director's career. Although they are indeed deeply Russian in spirit, these last three works are as international in outlook and appeal as they are in their literary sources. In 1957, then, Kozintsev directed a film based on Cervantes's literary classic, *Don Quixote.* Starring the great Soviet actor Nikolai Cherkasov, the film is a masterful example of discrete literary adaptation in cinema. It is especially memorable for its startling use of color, as well as for its quite elegant pictorial compositions. In the film, the Crimea metamorphoses into a space of the mind. In its visual power, the film sometimes recalls Velásquez. Moreover, in *Don Quixote,* the director returns—intertextually, as it were—to themes and techniques explored in the FEKS period: explicitly, the world of carnival as posited by Mikhail Bakhtin. Games and inversions—homo ludens—might be described as a central focus of this remarkable text. Read against the cinema of Socialist Realism, Kozintsev's *Don Quixote* is revealed as a daring work of art indeed. Writers like Shklovsky and Borges have posited strongly "modern" readings of Cervantes's masterpiece. So, too, Kozintsev discovers in *Don Quixote* adumbrations of the contemporary.

Kozintsev's two next films also provide "modern" readings of classic literary texts, for they are based on Shakespeare's tragedies, *Hamlet* and *King Lear*. These two films clearly stand among the most successful avatars of Shakespeare in the cinema. The film version of *Hamlet* reflects a long-term preoccupation of Kozintsev's with Shakespeare's play, a preoccupation dating back as far as the FEKS period. Visually, Kozintsev's film is an austere and even laconic work, shot in black and white. It is especially memorable for its shrewd solution to the aesthetic problem posed by the ghost, a major problem indeed for any filmmaker tempted to adapt the play to the screen. As opposed to Laurence Olivier's celebrated film version of the play—a version much admired by Kozintsev—this Soviet version stresses the explicitly political significations of the play. Thus, in his film, Kozintsev is quite clearly in accord with those men of the theater—such as Jan Kott or Peter Brook—who would make of Shakespeare "our contemporary."

This is also the case in the last film Kozintsev was to make, the visually stunning *King Lear*. This last work is noted for its wonderful landscapes which operate, perhaps, as Eliotic objective correlatives. Also to be mentioned is Kozintsev's unique interpretation of the role of the Fool in the text. Here, too, the world of carnival with its disorienting ludic activities dominates the text, suggesting an intertextual allusion to the director's earlier *avant-garde* style and concerns.

Thus, as we shall see in the chapters that follow, *Don Quixote, Hamlet,* and *King Lear*—taken as a unit—suggest an *oeuvre* that forms a single text, with the films of different phases as its components. In *Don Quixote, Hamlet,* and *King Lear,* the director glances at great works of the literary past, but also at his own aesthetic enterprise. These last three films constitute the director's final phase, which, retrospectively, rereads the *avant-garde* and Socialist Realist phases. At his death, then, Kozintsev was again at the height of his powers, having completed the three excellent films of the final phase. A last project, a cinematic glance at the world of Gogol, was left unrealized. It should be noted that Kozintsev's contribution to the cinema was not limited to his directorial efforts. Kozintsev also taught and wrote about film. Two volumes of his writings have appeared in English translation: *Shakespeare: Time and Conscience* (1966) and *King Lear: The Space of Tragedy* (1977).

2

The Factory of the Eccentric Actor

KOZINTSEV'S cinematic enterprise in the 1920s raises the issue of the artistic *avant-garde*. Specifically, what is the relationship between *avant-garde* art and radical politics? The question haunts our century. If formal radicalism is to be identified with political radicalism, what, then, are we to do with advanced artists of the political right, such as Louis-Ferdinand Céline or Ezra Pound? No one has yet satisfactorily answered the question. In his novel *The Real Life of Sebastian Knight,* Vladimir Nabokov has gone so far as to attack what he calls "the queer notion (mainly based on a muddle of terms) that there is a natural connection between extreme politics and extreme art."[1] Nevertheless, the advanced artistic forms of Soviet art of the 1920s did indeed operate in the precise context of the Revolution. And when the political situation altered under Stalin, artistic form altered as well. The work of Kozintsev and Trauberg permits a scrutiny of this larger aesthetic and ideological metamorphosis.

Broadly speaking, it may be said that, unlike the nineteenth-century Russian Realists who aimed to show what the world was like, the new Soviet *avant-garde* aimed to create the world anew. The British critic John Berger has pointed out that, in the West, we are accustomed to thinking of the artistic *avant-garde* as a movement of opposition; the experience of the Soviets in the period immediately following the Bolshevik seizure of power was quite different indeed. Here, the *avant-garde* artists' "social consciousness was affirmative rather than critical."[2] Like the Bolsheviks, the artists of the Revolution were preoccupied with the machine, which, in political and aesthetic theory, was to free man, rather than enslave him. The labor of man—with art as its paradigmatic instance—was no longer to be transformed into a

27

The Adventures of Octyabrina, *the first of the FEKS films.*

Leonid Trauberg, Sergei Yutkevitch, and Grigori Kozintsev in 1922

commodity. The sense of process, of creation—what was believed to be man's most human characteristic, his labor—was to be retrieved. Thus Soviet *avant-garde* art was an art of process. In his labor—in the enterprise of creation—man would at once operate to create a world and himself!

Perhaps it is Ferdinand Alquié who has managed to formulate what is the crucial question: "Why is the political thought called leftist linked to the most reactionary and old-fashioned cultural thought? Why does the revolt by which man rises against the constraints weighing him down seem incompatible with revolution?"[3] It might be said in response that, in the Soviet Union in the 1920s, artists managed to combine advanced technique *and* advanced politics. We may grant to Nabokov, perhaps, that the connection is not a necessary one; but it *is* a possible one. Indeed, the Stalinist move to dismantle the Soviet *avant-garde* testifies to the potency of the latter's synthesis of politics and art.

The Carnivalistic

In his seminal analysis of Dostoevsky, *Problems of Dostoevsky's Poetics,* the Soviet literary theorist Mikhail Bakhtin has noted that "the carnivalistic life is life drawn out of its usual rut, it is to a degree 'life turned inside out,' 'life the wrong way round,'"[4] Bakhtin proposes that "the laws, prohibitions and restrictions which determine the system and order of normal, i.e. non-carnival, life are for the period of carnival suspended; above all the hierarchical system and all the connected forms of fear, awe, piety, etiquette, etc. are suspended, i.e. everything that is determined by social-hierarchical inequality among people, or any other form of inequality, including age."[5] The outbreak of the Bolshevik Revolution may be said to have inaugurated precisely such a system of carnivalistic life for the Soviet artists and intellectuals. All of the rules and hierarchies of the past appeared to have been overthrown at a single blow, and something resembling the most ancient forms of carnival, in which the king is uncrowned and the slave becomes the master, came into being. Kozintsev himself has described the first years of the Revolution as "a sort of fair . . . going on in the middle of every privation."[6] And, indeed, the spirit of carnival reversals, the confrontation of impossible oppositions, the joyous sense of profound ambiguity described by Bakhtin permeate the early works of Kozintsev and Trauberg. Sergei Gerassimov has remarked that "FEKS rejected, overthrew and negated in every possible way pre-existing forms of theatrical art."[7] Bakhtin's critical notion of the carnivalistic permits us to comprehend the thrust of FEKS.

Perhaps only in a period of carnival license, in which the rules of age and experience no longer dominated, could such youngsters as Kozintsev, Trauberg, and the others have emerged so rapidly and so vigorously. It must be recalled that Kozintsev was sixteen and Trauberg nineteen at the outset of their activities under the banner of FEKS. In witty fashion, the artists of FEKS took as their motto a line from the American writer Mark Twain: "It's better to be a young June-bug than an old bird of paradise." As full-fledged members of the carnival of the period, the members of FEKS had no interest in the usual rut of pre-revolutionary academism. First of all, they were to constitute a "factory," not a school, an ordinary theater, or a studio. This distinction is crucial. Like their great hero the poet Mayakovsky, they thought of themselves as art "workers." This new attitude toward art may be understood in relation to the carnivalistic spirit of familiarity, in which things are no longer separated from each other, but mix in merry confrontation. Art, then, was no longer to be something apart, placed on a pedestal, but instead a part of life, another kind of work. The carnivalistic spirit sent the members of FEKS, along with other artists, into the streets, into the urban world of noise, smells, and other shocks, which, in turn, inspired them. In the streets, they plastered the walls of buildings with their posters, announcing the creation of a new factory, one for acting.

Thus the essential carnivalism of FEKS is a specifically revolutionary strategy. The films of Kozintsev and Trauberg of this period exuberantly challenge some of the dominant conventions and ideas of the past. Their *avant-garde* texts called into question and thereby displaced stale artistic devices and, by implication, modes of perception. In part, then, the revolutionary project of FEKS may be situated in that area which contemporary criticism calls "intertextuality"—or, quite simply, the interactions among texts. Gerassimov, for instance, has recalled the manner in which FEKS situated its activities in relation to American film: "We were then infatuated with the American cinema. Detective films, burlesques, melodrama and of course all the films of Griffith were for us revelations and models. More exactly, we were inspired to re-do them better, according to our own fashion."[8] Here, the text is not rejected; instead, it becomes a model for new textual production.

Contemporary theories of intertextuality generally evoke the ideas of the Russian Formalist critics such as Victor Shklovsky and Yuri Tynianov, who—not surprisingly—were among the most supportive and perceptive of Kozintsev and Trauberg's early critics. As the Russian Formalist critics well understood, the artist engages in a revision and a critique of his medium. Although this is, in essence, *always* the case, the *avant-garde* artist does so perhaps most explicitly of all. In this perspective, the work of art is always, in a sense, also a work of criticism—of other works of art. As Shklovsky put it in a well-known formulation: "The work of art arises from the background of other works and through association with them. The form of a work of art is defined by its relation to other works of art, to forms existing prior to it."[9] Thus, in his essay on FEKS, Shklovsky underscores the group's attention to its own materials. In this concern, a given artistic production of FEKS operated in terms of other artistic texts. These other texts were not only films, but novels, paintings, and popular art forms, too. The aim of this tactic was to set the mind of the spectator into motion, to challenge stale ways of thinking.

In an excellent critical text on *The New Babylon*, Bernard Eisenschitz has alluded to Kozintsev and Trauberg's use of "citations" in their films.[10] These allusions to cinematic and other artistic texts play a theoretical role. The work of art assumes a reflexive stance. Eisenschitz suggests the manner in which Kozintsev and Trauberg engage in a critique of cinematic transparence, the illusion of reality. Eisenschitz usefully compares their conception of the medium to Eisenstein's notion of "intellectual cinema." Eisenstein's sense of montage as collision is frequently contrasted by film historians to Pudovkin's sense of it as linkage. Eisenschitz correctly aligns Kozintsev and Trauberg with the former approach, which is, of course, far more radical in its implications. Indeed, collision on the *aesthetic* plane might be taken to reflect collision, or indeed, by implication, revolution, on the *political*. The particular collision encountered in the FEKS films of Kozintsev and Trauberg is generally one of styles, ideas, and modes of perception. It is in this sense that Kozintsev and Trauberg may indeed be said to operate within the domain of "intellectual cinema."

The FEKS manifesto generally functioned to announce the group's break with the past—its collisions with the stale and worn-out. In addition to its strategies of shock, the FEKS retrieval of popular art forms served to mark off its production from works of the past. Bakhtin has pointed out that "eccentricity is a special category of the carnival attitude which is organically connected with the category of familiar contact; it permits the latent sides of human nature to be revealed and developed in a concretely sensuous form."[11] In this regard, one might well turn to the anthology of manifestos published by FEKS in 1922. The fundamental attitude of the young *avant-garde* artists was the contestation of the norm. The eccentric style aimed at subverting the automatic acceptance of the world as it is. Bakhtin usefully suggests the dialogical character of the eccentric, its self-questioning. The work, then, enters into a dialogue with other works, precisely the FEKS strategy.

Reading Gogol

The first theatrical production of FEKS, in 1922, was a highly radical reading of Gogol's *Marriage*, which they called *A Gag in Three Acts: The Electrification of Gogol*. The title suggests the explicitly eccentric approach to the text taken by these young men of the theater. We might wonder about the choice of Gogol in this regard. After all, if a basic premise of the *avant-garde* artists under consideration here was a rejection of the art of the past, what, then, were Kozintsev, Trauberg, and their friends doing with Gogol, a figure from the Russian literary canon? Their Gogol, however, was one who suited the needs of their own *avant-garde* enterprise. Kozintsev would later write that "in the years of our youth Gogol seemed one of us, the most 'left' man in art, as we used to say."[12] The particular Gogol seized upon by the artists of FEKS was the writer of "unlikely happenings," as Kozintsev put it, that is, the Gogol who juxtaposed unlikely or unrelated objects and events. This tactic of juxtaposition is, of course, an important feature of Bakhtin's notion of the carnivalistic. Indeed, the strategy of taking something out of its context and placing it elsewhere, which Kozintsev encountered in Gogol, later earned FEKS the label of "Formalist."

Both the FEKS artists and the Russian Formalists placed special emphasis on techniques for detaching a thing from its context and juxtaposing it with something entirely unexpected. It was, in fact, a dictum of Russian Formalist criticism that art exists to "make strange" or "defamiliarize" our perceptions of the everyday world. Said Shklovsky: "Art exists that one may recover the sensation of life; it exists to make me feel things, to make the stone stony. The purpose of art is to impart the sensation of things as they are perceived and not as they are known. The technique of art is to make objects 'unfamiliar,' to make forms difficult, to increase the difficulty and length of perception because the process of perception is an aesthetic end in itself and must be prolonged."[13] For Russian Formalist criticism, the automaticity of response is to be subverted by art so that objects may be perceptible once more. Literary historians frequently point to the fact that the Russian Formalist critics did not operate in isolation, but, rather, in relation to actual artistic practice. Indeed, works of the Russian Formalists—Shklovsky's *Third Factory* and *Zoo, or Letters Not About Love* are excellent examples—frequently oscillated between literary criticism and art itself. It should not be surprising, then, that FEKS shared something of a community of aspiration with Russian Formalism. We may say, perhaps, that in their reading of texts of the past, FEKS aimed at defamiliarizing them, making them perceptible once more. It must be recalled, after all, that this was to be an "electrification" of Gogol's text! "It was," Kozintsev has recalled, "a case of trying to demolish all the usual theatrical forms and to find others, which would create the intense sentiment of the new life."[14]

What were the aesthetic aspirations of the early theatrical production of FEKS? Evidently, they aimed to capture some of the spirit which, according to Gorky, Lenin had discovered in the music halls of London. Kozintsev, in one of his texts, evokes the following perception of Lenin's: "Here there is a sort of satirical or skeptical relationship to what is commonly accepted, there is a striving to turn it inside out . . . to show the illogicality of the ordinary."[15] Lenin's perception was of great interest to Kozintsev, for it might be taken to refer to some of the fundamental tactics of FEKS, as well. The rationale for the use of disjunctive strategies was that the connections between actions might be distorted, thereby defamiliarizing experience. Thus the early productions of FEKS are legendary for their reputed speed, their use of hyperbole, and a certain roughness. Here is how Kozintsev recalls one of their productions: "We wanted to show everything: people blown up like posters, cascades of gags, a combination of real-life actors playing in front of the screen. We gathered bits and pieces without ever thinking what the whole effect would be. . . . We had extracted some bits of a Chaplin film—I do not remember which; the copy was incomplete. While the film was projected on the screen, in front, in the foreground, the actors played. Some characters were dressed in the 'constructivist' style—no doubt under the influence of Picasso's designs for *Parade*."[16] Thus it would seem that all of the elements of the production were to confront each other in a festive profusion of eccentric carnivalism. The Chaplin footage is sundered from its context and assumes new meaning in its collision with extracinematic elements. In this regard, Kozintsev's attention to the collision of multiple fragments is particularly interesting; its aim would appear to be a stunning shock effect, of the sort proposed by Walter Benjamin in his theoretical writings.

Degraded Forms

In manifesto form, FEKS argued for an "art without a capital letter, without a pedestal, and without a figleaf." Here, their aspiration was to demystify art. For this young *avant-garde,* museums, cathedrals, and libraries belonged to yesterday. Art was now to be reintegrated into everyday life in the modern world. Kozintsev has since remarked upon the great irony of this early rejection of the canons of the past, when, years later, in his maturity, he would turn to quite traditional art, as incarnated in Shakespeare's *Hamlet* and *King Lear,* for the sources for films. Indeed, the impulse during the FEKS period was quite different. The inspiration for their projects was often discovered in the realm of what Russian Formalist criticism called "degraded forms." Thus, for instance, it was the poster, rather than the oil painting, which inspired aspects of their earliest work. And, as in the case of much *avant-garde* activity of the period, the circus and the boxing match were seized upon for material.

Writing about this aesthetic appropriation of other sorts of material, Shklovsky remarked that "literature extends its boundaries, annexing non-aesthetic material. This material, and the changes which it undergoes through contact with the material already aesthetically processed, must be taken into account."[17] Of course, this operation was to be recognized as a law of the other arts, as well. Quite explicitly, Shklovsky's dictum was an essential component of the FEKS approach. FEKS delighted in the appropriation of nonaesthetic material. This material, however, was altered in its new context. As Shklovsky explains the process theoretically: ". . . artistic form carries out its own unique rape of the Sabine women. The material ceases to recognize its former lord and master. Once processed by the law of art, it can be perceived apart from its place of origin."[18] Thus, although FEKS proposed an art which defined itself through intimate contact with life itself, it would be an error to suppose that these artists were engaging in a simple populism. In the work of FEKS, popular, "degraded" forms were to take on a new life and participate in the production of new meanings. In juxtaposition with unexpected other sources, an assemblage would be produced which "made strange" its various components. The logic of the familiar was to have no place in the early productions of FEKS.

Thus, elements from such areas as the circus, the cabaret, the music hall, and the sports arena collided in the *avant-garde* world of FEKS. Accounts of the early productions stress the ellipsis and discontinuity which marked them. Indeed, an emphasis upon fragmentary, nonlinear effects appeared to suit the particular historical context in which FEKS operated, one of revolution and general upheaval. The conflict of the period was to find itself reflected in an aesthetic of conflict. As it evolved in the 1920s, the celebrated FEKS style "laid bare"—as the Russian Formalists would say—its broken, episodic forms. No attempt was made, it seems, to efface gaps or fractures. This effacement would later be a tactic of Socialist Realist art in its struggle to evolve "transparent" texts which provided the illusion of reality. For FEKS, on the contrary, the fundamental strategy was a reflexive one: to "lay bare" the artistic device.

At the time of the first FEKS production, Kozintsev and Trauberg were visited by another young man who would become a major force in the Soviet cinema. Thus Kozintsev has recalled a memorable presence at the premiere of the Gogol piece, "a young man with a huge forehead and a lot of hair."[19] It was, of course, Sergei Eisenstein, who proceeded to shout, "Too slow! Much too slow! Speed up the action!" Eisenstein's biographer, Yon Barna, has reported that Kozintsev told him that the FEKS production of Gogol's *Marriage,* which Eisenstein attended, influenced the latter's production of an Ostrovsky play, which he presented in Moscow the following year. Barna points out that Eisenstein's encounter with FEKS influenced "his own theatrical thinking." After this important encounter, Eisenstein returned to Moscow with Yutkevitch, where they hoped to advance the notions evolved by FEKS. Of course, Eisenstein shared with FEKS such mutual influences as Meyerhold and Mayakovsky, so that the strong effect on him of this encounter with Kozintsev and Trauberg is not surprising. Kozintsev pointed out to Barna the manner in which the FEKS manifesto concerning the "chain of tricks," which appeared in December 1921, was followed two years later by Eisenstein's manifesto concerning the "montage of attractions." Kozintsev, however, stressed to Barna that "there was certainly no question of plagiarism; all these ideas were in the air."[20] This meeting of Eisenstein and FEKS is of particular interest, because it demonstrates the manner in which *avant-garde* notions were indeed "in the air" at this time.

The Lure of Film

Both Eisenstein, on the one hand, and Kozintsev and Trauberg, on the other, were to move from *avant-garde* theater to cinema. Although Kozintsev continued to work in the *theater* for the rest of his life, after 1924 he and Trauberg became major figures in the evolving Soviet cinema. The two young and now "experienced" artists were all of nineteen and twenty-two, respectively, when Sevzapkino, one of the small production groups, accepted their first film script. The project, an "eccentric comedy," was to become the film entitled *The Adventures of Oktyarbrina,* featuring Z. Tarkhovskaya and Sergei Martinson. The Russian Formalist writer Yuri Tynianov has written the following about the film:

Their first film, which probably few remember, but which the FEKS's love like a first-born child, was *The Adventures of Oktyabrina.* This small film, which was made under heaven knows what conditions, does not belong among the important films of any genre. The *Adventures* made liberal use of all the tricks that the FEKS people had been panting to utilize once they entered that paradise—the cinema. The least pretentious episode I remember from it is a crowd bicyling across roofs! Nevertheless the FEKS's are right to love their *Oktyabrina*. It taught them not about "monumental epics" or "fundamental comics," where there were already footprints to guide them, but it helped them to discover, even to invent, elements of cinema, and without excess timidity they snatched at that thing around which more respectful and less quick-witted had erected taboos: the cinema as an art.[21]

Tynianov's evocative comments suggest vividly the excitement which Kozintsev and Trauberg must have felt as they entered the "paradise" of filmmaking. Russian Formalist criticism was especially sensitive to the role of devices in art. Tynianov indicates, then, the particular attraction cinematic devices held for the young *avant-garde* artists who composed FEKS. Debates concerning the specificity of the cinema—its special means of expression—usually focus on its vocabulary of devices. These, perhaps, are the "tricks" to which Tynianov alludes. The critic's remarks give us an idea of the field of possibilities that extended before the young filmmakers. Their lack of "respect"—their iconoclasm—permitted them access to this field. Since the film appears to exist in only a single copy, we must rely on Kozintsev's own description of it:

. . . *The Adventures of Oktyabrina* was a sort of propaganda film-poster: the influence of the propaganda plays and the Rosta windows shows clearly in every moment of the film. The capitalistic shark has been introduced to Petrograd and demands repayment of the Tsarist debits by the peasants and the workers. The shark wore a silk hat; he was played by Sergei Martinson (whose first role it was), with no make-up apart from enormous black velvet eyebrows. Hearing of the arrival of Coolidge Curzonovitch Poincare (the name of the shark), the NEP-man, in a fashionable check suit, lets himself go. The plots of this duo are foiled by the young komsomol girl Oktyabrina. . . . The young girl, wearing a felt hat with a star of the Red army, puts things to right, and continues the struggle against the survivals of the past.

Kozintsev alludes here to major artistic influences drawn from the realm of popular culture. Rosta, the telegraphic agency, caught the attention of the young Kozintsev immediately after his arrival in Petrograd. Kozintsev has described his encounter with the Rosta windows at 25 October Prospect. Initially curious because of the crowd lingering there, Kozintsev found himself quite interested in the so-called "manuscript bulletins." Moreover, "collage posters" also to be found there struck the young Kozintsev with their energetic approach and form. The quoted passage already suggests the manner in which the films of FEKS would be essentially nonnaturalistic in technique. Kozintsev continues:

All these characters seemed directly descended from the propaganda lorry which entertained the populace at the May Day parade. It was all rather disconnected, but galloped along on the screen, full of dizzying abridgements of the story and shock cuts. And when the narrative got stuck, letters would appear on the screen: dancing about in the manner of cartoon films, they would group themselves into words, forming slogans that were then familiar.[22]

Today, Kozintsev's lively account of the film provides us with some idea of the manner in which the energetic *avant-garde* style of FEKS was transported from theater to cinema. In particular, we note Kozintsev's stress upon "dizzying abridgements of the story and shock cuts." Techniques of temporal and spatial ellipsis are frequently encountered in the later films of FEKS, as well as in other examples of the cinematic *avant-garde*. Such vertiginous effects operate as marked elements, disorienting us, frustrating our expectations.

The circumstances of Kozintsev and Trauberg's cinematic debut are curious indeed. Unable to gain access to the first studios they approached, the young Kozintsev and Trauberg found themselves directed to the offices of Sevzapkino, where two marginal Pathé cameras constituted the resources. Kozintsev has recalled that the tone of Sevzapkino suggested the cinema of the prerevolutionary period. It existed quite oddly out of touch with the artistic and social whirlwinds swirling about it. Kozintsev's memory quite cinematically focused upon certain

synecdochal details encountered in the office of Sevzapkino:
postcards depicting "reproductions of antique statues, portraits
by Repin, and photographs of ancient coaches in the Stable
Museum." The details suggest fragments of the artistic past. This
was the very sort of art displaced by the *avant-garde* movement.
Kozintsev is suggesting that the films of Sevzapkino emerge from
such an aesthetic context. Repin postcards, perhaps, glance back
toward the past and, ironically, ahead toward Socialist Realism.
Against this background, it was for filmmakers like Kozintsev and
Trauberg to invent cinema!

It may seem odd that, even under revolutionary conditions,
such utter freedom would be given to two youngsters working on
their first film. Kozintsev has recalled that, in fact, this degree of
freedom came about quite by accident. It seems that an
experienced director had been assigned to the film. When he
realized that their film's shooting would take place "on the
sloping roof of a very tall building," he decided not to attend.
And when he discovered that their next set-up would be "from
the sphere of the Admiralty building, shooting from just below
the weather vane," he disappeared from the production
entirely.[23] Thus Kozintsev and Trauberg found themselves on
their own—and were quite happy to be so!

During the period of its early work in cinema, FEKS strived to
perfect its approach to the problems of acting. Gerassimov has
described the training which took place in the mansion on
Gagarinskaya Street, which FEKS had been given for its
activities. Following the important example of Meyerhold's
system of biomechanics, the actors involved with Kozintsev and
Trauberg received a comprehensive athletic training. They
studied boxing, acrobatics, and gymnastics as preparation for
their acting tasks. Trauberg operated as the theoretician for the
group, while Kozintsev taught the notion of "cine-gesture." This
notion, essential to the evolving FEKS style, was "based on the
mathematical precision of American comic and detective films.
The actor was required not to 'feel.' The word 'feeling' was only
ever pronounced with derisive grimaces accompanied by scorn-
ful laughter from the whole troupe." Gerassimov played a role
in the second film of Kozintsev and Trauberg, *Mishka Against
Yudenitch,* and recalls it as "an accumulation of the most
audacious tricks, dizzy falls, the maddest inventions." According

to Gerassimov, the film was largely improvised, its scenario "written on a little scrap of paper."[24]

First Success

In 1925, Eisenstein's cinematic debut, *Strike*, was released. After viewing it with great interest, Kozintsev announced to his friends that "all that we've been doing up to now is baby stuff. We have to review our whole fashion of thinking, everything."[25] *Strike* was, of course, to have a monumental impact on the world cinema in general. As we can see in Kozintsev's words, it *immediately* affected those closest to it, Eisenstein's colleagues in the evolving Soviet cinema. In March 1926, the first result of the impact of *Strike* on FEKS was screened; it was called *The Devil's Wheel*. With this superb film, Kozintsev and Trauberg put their name on the map of world cinema. It was, Tynianov remarked, a first success for the partners, and animated much debate among the Leningrad critics. Writing in 1928, the Soviet critic Vladimir Nedobrovo pointed out that, in *The Devil's Wheel*, quotidian life is the material utilized by the filmmakers, while eccentrism is their technique.[26] This synthesis remains an impressive achievement.

The film involves the story of a young sailor from a battleship named *Aurora*. He meets a pretty girl at an amusement park while he is on shore leave with his buddies. The sailor succumbs to the double lure of the pretty girl and the amusement park atmosphere and overstays his leave. As a deserter, he is easy prey for a gang of petty criminals who lurk about the park. These dubious characters trick the two young people into joining the underworld. The sailor, however, is finally able to gather the necessary resolve to turn himself in and aid the militia with the information necessary to break up the gang.

Kozintsev has repeatedly stressed the "happy" quality of the artistic production of the Soviet *avant-garde* of the 1920s. This quality is precisely that festive spirit of the carnivalistic, which Bakhtin has sketched. FEKS rejected the serious tones of tragedy; its world was one of joyous subversion! The locale of *The Devil's Wheel*, an amusement park, is significant in this regard. It suggests a play-world, a space marked off for ludic activity. Like Eisenstein and Yutkevitch, Kozintsev and

Sergei Gerassimov in *The Devil's Wheel*

Trauberg were fascinated by the attractions to be discovered in amusement parks. Indeed, the same attractions which provided inspiration for Eisenstein's early notions of montage, were equally influential on Kozintsev and Trauberg's idea of eccentrism.

In *The Devil's Wheel*, Kozintsev and Trauberg appropriate the amusement-park locale in order to create an alternate world, an eccentric locus of playful subversion. In the amusement park, the logic and meaning of the everyday world are suspended. The park is inhabited by players and filled with devices which quite literally subvert stability—such as roller coasters and spinning wheels. Disoriented by the camera's breakneck rides—plunging down on the rails of the roller coaster, spinning around on the tilted surface of the "devil's wheel"—the film's spectator finds himself in another world. Mr. Question—brilliantly played by Gerassimov—rules this strange play-world. Mr. Question is a magician—or, more accurately, he is a petty gangster playing a part. Within the film's diegesis, then, Gerassimov's character has two faces; identity has become play, a play of fictions. This is an eccentric space of ambiguity, to be sure. Even the stability of self is called into question.

A sense of otherness is prominent in *The Devil's Wheel*. It is most powerfully suggested in the disturbing appearance of real freaks as inhabitants of the amusement park. The use of freaks in the film may be read as another tactic of the carnivalistic subversion or contestation of the norm. Moreover, the overall appropriation of the stylized, acrobatic movements of the circus intensifies this essential contestation. We are perhaps most intensely aware of such movement in the film in that remarkable scene during the final police attack, when the members of the gang fall out of the windows of the abandoned building which serves as their hideout. Remarkably, they tumble from the ledges like a swarm of clowns descending to the sawdust. Quotidian life shatters; we find ourselves in the topsy-turvy world of the carnivalistic.

The ruin of an abandoned building is systematically utilized in *The Devil's Wheel*. Like Meyerhold's famous sets, this is a kind of machine for acting. As the initial shot of the building appears, people suddenly materialize in the empty windows, as if by magic—recalling, perhaps, the materializations in Eisenstein's *Strike*. Indeed, throughout the film, Kozintsev and Trauberg play with the magical properties of the medium. This play may be as simple as utilizing slow motion as a marked element in relation to normal speed. Elsewhere, the screen itself is split into sections, the world split asunder. Kozintsev was later to remark upon the preoccupation with rhythm which characterized this period of artistic effort. Thus, in contrast to what later developed in Socialist Realist films such as *The Youth of Maxim.* the early works of Kozintsev and Trauberg focused on movement, rhythm, and sheer cinematic manipulation, rather than on psychology.

Filming Gogol

An index of the truly remarkable productivity of FEKS during this period was the release of another film that same year, *The Cloak*, based on Gogol. As they had in their earlier theatrical period, Kozintsev and Trauberg now turned once again to this figure from the Russian literary canon. Again, for Kozintsev, Gogol was "the most 'left' man in art." This notion is interesting because it reveals the very specific conception of Gogol reflected in the film. In their reading of Gogol, then, Kozintsev and Trauberg had to pick and choose those elements in the text which suited their conception. Those elements which did not lend themselves to the FEKS notion of an "electrified" Gogol were, of course, repressed. Kozintsev was to remark that they "had to separate his gay elements from his naturalistic grayness . . . so that the 'unlikely happenings' should come alive, so that the world could fall apart. . . ."[27] Thus Kozintsev and Trauberg's film suggests a new reading of a classic text. Adaptation becomes an intertextual operation, the reading of one text through another.

Indeed, the Gogol encountered in the FEKS film was considered a radical departure from the traditional reading of this author which had dominated Russian critical discourse since the time of the so-called Radical Critics of the nineteenth century. Motivated by a view of literature as a weapon for animating and achieving social change, the Radical Critics envisioned Gogol as one of the great Russian realists. This champion of the little man was an author who used naturalistic literary technique in order to unveil the injustices of tsarist Russia. Clearly, this is not the Gogol whom we encounter in Kozintsev and Trauberg's reading. In fact, it is precisely *against*

Andrei Kostrichkin as Akaky Akakiyevich Bashmachkin in *The Cloak*

this approach that Kozintsev and Trauberg's interpretation may be understood. Thus the filmmakers firmly rejected the realist Gogol proposed by the Radical Critics. The Gogol of the FEKS film *The Cloak* suggests the author encountered in the writings of the Russian Formalists—especially Boris Eikhenbaum in his celebrated essay "How Gogol's *Overcoat* is made." The Gogol proposed by the Russian Formalists was no Critical Realist! Stylistic play and the use of grotesques to undermine referentiality are the characteristics of this *other,* Formalist Gogol.

The screenplay for *The Cloak* was written by the Formalist author Tynianov. As the basis for his script, Tynianov mixed two Gogol texts, "Nevsky Prospect" and "The Cloak" (or "The Overcoat"). A certain slightness of story is characteristic of much of Gogol's work. In fact, Gogol did not even make up his own stories, but borrowed them from friends, including Pushkin. As the film by Kozintsev and Trauberg develops, we note substantial variations from its literary sources. But it does share with Gogol's texts a noticeably slight plot interest. Indeed, its fascination lies elsewhere.

In the first part of *The Cloak,* an insignificant St. Petersburg copying clerk, Akaky Akakievich Bashmachkin, is encountered as a young man. While walking on the Nevsky Prospect, he glimpses a beautiful woman, whom he does not recognize as a prostitute. Thus he becomes hopelessly infatuated with her. The prostitute, however, has only one interest in Akaky Akakievich: she wants to use his skills as a copyist in order to alter the signature on a legal summons for one of her friends. In the second part of the film, Akaky Akakievich is no longer a young man. Like his dreams, his cloak has now grown tattered and threadbare, and his entire existence now revolves around his endless copying, which he relentlessly pursues day and night. Yet—briefly— Akaky Akakievich seems to come to life once more when, having saved his rubles by the most desperate economies, he manages to purchase a new cloak for himself. Unfortunately, his moments of happiness are abruptly ended when a gang of thieves accosts him in a deserted, snow-covered Petersburg square in order to steal his cloak. In a frenzy, Akaky Akakievich summons the courage to approach a certain "important person" for help in recovering his cherished possession. The "important person" is offended that Akaky Akakievich would dare to approach him directly, and therefore refuses to give him any assistance. Finding no recourse, in the end, Akaky Akakievich falls into a delirium and dies.

Thus, as in the Gogol texts on which it is based, the film is without overwhelming events. Where, then, does its great interest lie? Surely, Kozintsev and Trauberg were not making a documentary of the trivial life of a poor Petersburg clerk in the interest of social justice. Indeed, nothing could be more distant from the fundamental impulse of *The Cloak*. Nor do Kozintsev and Trauberg seek to provide us with a conventional psychological analysis of the downtrodden little fellow. If Akaky Akakievich is understood by the spectator of this film, it is not through conventional psychological analysis, but, rather, through explicitly cinematic strategies, such as complex plays on scale and perspective, in which the figure of the little man is dwarfed against the giant objects and landscapes.

As the city is photographed here to accentuate rather than attenuate the overall atmosphere of fantasy, so, too, objects function in a fantastic manner. It is the cloak itself which operates as a consummate example of the way in which inanimate objects appear to possess a life of their own and ultimately come to dominate Akaky Akakievich. The cloak seems somehow to fascinate the camera eye, just as it obsesses Akaky Akakievich. It may be remarked that the tightly framed shots of this fetishized object operate—within the context of Kozintsev's *oeuvre* as a whole—in marked contrast to Kozintsev and Trauberg's use of the close-up in a Socialist Realist film like *The Youth of Maxim*. In *The Cloak* the close-up functions to disorient the spectator, who finds himself deprived of a coherent space. Of course, this disjunctive, *avant-garde* tactic was to be abandoned in the Socialist Realist period when *The Youth of Maxim* would be made. In *The Cloak*, the camera is often so close to the cloak itself that the audience is metaphorically suffocated by the object, much as Akaky Akakievich himself is. *The Cloak*, then, operates within the context of a cinema of poetry, with its stress on metaphor as opposed to metonymy.

Kozintsev and Trauberg conceived of *The Cloak* as "a fantasy on the theme of Gogol." Indeed, its setting—the notorious, mythic city of Petersburg, which was known to drive men mad with its infamous "White Nights"—was a perfect space for fantasy. The film's world is, essentially, the subjectivity of the copying clerk, Akaky Akakievich. The camera seizes upon the city of Petersburg as Akaky Akakievich perceives it. Thus, once again, as in many Russian works before it, Petersburg metamorphoses into a city of the imagination. Particularly for non-Russian audiences, it is quite essential to recall immediately the subtle aura which has surrounded this remarkable city from the time it was first built on the swamps of the Neva at a great cost in human life. Peter the Great needed a window on the West to serve his goals for the westernization and modernization of Russia. He selected a site for his new capital close to Finland, and there, on the festering swamplands, he built his city of the mind. Petersburg's plan is one of utter rationality. Its severe and beautiful geometry contrasts sharply with the natural surroundings over which it was imposed. Since the days of Peter, then, few cities have been written about so passionately and so effectively. Gogol, of course, but also Pushkin, Dostoevsky, and Andrei Biely created powerful literary images of it. Indeed, so often has it been the object of artistic scrutiny—and by the very greatest of writers—that Petersburg may justifiably be thought of as a literary city, a mental locale. Kozintsev and Trauberg's treatment of it in *The Cloak* must be comprehended within the rich context of the literary conception of Petersburg as it has cut across Russian writing. The city which we encounter upon the screen in the course of *The Cloak* no more existed in reality than did Akaky Akakievich. It must be stressed that *The Cloak* does not set out as a recording or reflection of reality—the aim of so-called Realist works—but, rather, it operates to rework those already constituted aesthetic images of the city which suggest its mythic character.

The Cloak is dominated by various devices of "ostranenie," the Formalist term for "making strange." Formalist criticism appears to utilize the idea of "making strange" in two ways. Sometimes, "making strange" seems to refer to artistic devices employed in the text. Worn-out, automatized devices—once marked elements which had become unmarked through extensive use—had to be replaced by new devices. Other times, "making strange" alludes to the world itself, which art operated to make perceptible again. We may say that in Kozintsev and Trauberg's *The Cloak*, both form *and* content are "made strange." Notably, the world in which Akaky Akakievich lives is filled with various subversive, parodic doubles. In *The Cloak,* the reverse of the usual may become the norm—in carnivalistic fashion. Everything is contested by its parodic double. For instance, the juxtaposition and joining of two fundamentally disjunct images—a woman and an overcoat—result in the phenomenon which Bakhtin describes as "the creation of a double which discrowns its counterpart."[28] Indeed, our expectations are violated in this manner throughout the film, as dummies, teapots, and other objects are metamorphosed into the carnivalistic parodies of the human.

The dreamy city through which Akaky Akakievich moves from day to day threatens to swallow him up. In a particularly unsettling reversal, the central figure of this film is not really a man at all, but, rather, a cloak! Man is seen to be dominated by inanimate objects. Kozintsev and Trauberg provide us with a powerful drama of reification. Indeed, while FEKS was criticized for the film's alleged lack of social consciousness, we can hardly imagine a more incisive analysis of reification, as proposed by Karl Marx in *The Economic and Philosophic Manuscripts of 1844.* In the first part of the film, the young clerk has a human object for his erotic desire, but, in the second part, all eroticism has been displaced onto the cloak. Sensuous lighting causes the fur to glisten, duplicating the image which the poor fellow no doubt possesses in his thoughts. When Akaky Akakievich hangs his beloved cloak on a peg in the cloakroom in his office, the camera pans down its surface as if it were a voluptuous nude. It would seem that it is only when covered with his cloak that Akaky Akakievich exists in the world. The social interest of *The Cloak,* then, lies in its chronicle of Akaky Akakievich's dehumanization.

After he first receives the cloak from the tailor's hands, we watch as he proudly walks the streets of Petersburg, people extending greetings to him as he passes. We soon realize, however, that it is actually not the poor copyist who is being greeted, but, rather, the cloak, which literally conceals his tiny body within it. This suspicion is confirmed by the party which his coworkers give, less for him than for his cloak. Thus, as long as Akaky Akakievich wears his cloak, his fellow clerks surround him and take notice. When a servant takes the cloak from him, however, he soon feels out of place and becomes quite invisible for the others. It must be noted, of course, that the cloak is not the only object to subvert or dominate the human world in the film. In addition, gestures and parts of the body often appear to detach themselves in a startling tactic of defamiliarization.

A significant confusion between the living and the inert occurs in the sequence in the tailor shop, where Akaky Akakievich goes initially in hopes of having his old, tattered coat repaired. There, he mistakes a coat on a manikin for a person. He speaks of it as if it were alive, and, by its position in the composition of the shot, the audience may share some of the Akaky Akakievich's confusion. Placed in the extreme left foreground of the shot, it immediately captures the viewer's eye by appearing larger than anything else. Then, when the camera takes in the tailor himself, it is not the man who captures the viewer's interest, but his foot, or, even more specifically, the gestures of the big toe. The foot— and the gestures of the toe—are thus oddly defamiliarized. Through the tactic of "making strange," the foot itself becomes a prop, almost as if it were detached from its human source, the tailor. Indeed, both the tailor and his wife utilize gestures and movements which seem more appropriate to a circus acrobat. Of course, this is the acrobatic FEKS style of acting operating to carnivalize the scene.

Thus Akaky Akakievich finds himself adrift in a world of menacing objects. Often placed at an angle above the figure of the poor copyist, the camera shows the scale of the buildings whose imperious facades serve to dwarf him. Towering statues also emphasize the dominance of the inanimate forms. This dominance is underscored when the copyist interprets a statue's "gesture"—its extended arm—as an order to him to go to see the important person after the theft of the cloak. And, indeed, if only for a moment, a command actually seems to emanate from this figure of stone. Shadows also serve to unleash an array of doubles. For instance, the figures of the robbers—like that of Akaky Akakievich himself early in the film—are first seen as approaching shadows. In this world of doubles, reality and fantasy contest each other, so as to create a thoroughly ambiguous situation in which distinctions are blurred.

The tension between the animate and the inert is superbly realized in a sequence involving a process of transformation. When Akaky Akakievich is saving for his new cloak, he dispenses with eating as one of his economy measures. Thus he falls under the sway of a remarkable vision. In it, the old cloak, covered with patches and quite tattered indeed, is hanging in his room.

Suddenly, it not only comes alive and gets down off the hook to approach Akaky Akakievich, but it also metamorphoses into a new cloak, luxurious and splendid. Then, as if this initial metamorphosis were not enough to delight the now smiling clerk, yet another transformation occurs, as the cloak metamorphoses into a woman, the prostitute with whom he was so infatuated in the first section of the film. In this metamorphosis, we witness not simply an extreme situation of alienation, but a fascinating displacement of erotic desire. The displacement of desire from the woman to the cloak is *realized* poetically in this dream sequence. Here, the cloak is not simply depicted as coming alive, but as being *like* a woman. When the tailor places the cloak on the shoulders of Akaky Akakievich, the latter trembles as if in the midst of an erotic experience. After all, the dream sequence has clearly suggested the erotic status of the cloak. Hence, when the garment is stolen from the clerk, it is not simply a mere object that has been lost. Not only has it conveyed a new importance upon him in the eyes of others, but it has also existed in an erotic relationship with him. The loss of the cloak is an erotic loss, a loss of love.

The final section of *The Cloak* contains another of Akaky Akakievich's remarkable visions. Having been harshly ejected by the important person who has refused his request for assistance in recovering the cloak, the poor copyist takes to his bed, where yet another vision overtakes him. In his fevered state, he seems to perceive a hideous grotesque crouched at his feet at the edge of the bed: the important person himself! As Akaky Akakievich stares up at the apparition, the latter thumbs his nose at the figure beneath him on the bed. In this scandalous—perhaps even Dostoevskian—gesture, the poor copyist's death is robbed of human dignity. The gesture is, of course, stylized in the eccentric mode.

In his delirium Akaky Akakievich climbs up a ladder. Provoked by the important person, he tumbles back into a totally new space, landing on the table in his office. An army of his fellow clerks is seated around the desk. At once they proceed to take up their quills and stab him to death with them. In this brutal fantasy, we may discover a visual pun: Akaky Akakievich dies by the pen. Indeed, a moment later, in a variant of this scene, Akaky Akakievich, still in his room, rises from his bed in order to take up his quill and write his death notice. This emphasis on writing may be taken to suggest the fundamental artifice of the life and death of Akaky Akakievich. This final moment suggests, perhaps, the status of *The Cloak* as antirealist and reflexive in its approach to filmic narrative, as well as to the Gogol text upon which it is based. *The Cloak* remains a stunning achievement of the FEKS style.

Film and History

Kozintsev and Trauberg released two FEKS films in 1927, *The Little Brother* and *S.V.D., or The Club of the Big Deed*. Critically rejected by Tynianov, *The Little Brother* has been recalled as a lyrical comedy about a chauffeur who decides to repair and restore a truck. With *S.V.D., or The Club of the Big Deed*, however, Kozintsev and Trauberg once more contributed substantially to the history of the medium. Its script was written by Tynianov in collaboration with Y. Oksman and dealt with the nineteenth-century Decembrist uprising. Tynianov liked to view films intertextually, that is, in relation to other films. Thus, for instance, *The Cloak* was to be situated intertextually in relation to a 1925 film by Yuri Zheliabuzhsky, *The Station Master*, which was based on a Pushkin text. Kozintsev and Trauberg's *The Cloak* offered an alternate solution to the problem of the cinematic adaptation of classic literary texts. Its solution, then, functioned intertextually in relation to Zheliabuzhsky's film. Similarly, for Tynianov, *S.V.D., or The Club of the Big Deed* operated intertextually in relation to another film, Alexander Ivanovski's *The Decembrists* (1926). Ivanovski's film suggested the conventions of the traditional historical costume film. These conventions are subverted in the Kozintsev and Trauberg text, which offers a highly eccentric approach to the problems of the historical film. Ironically, its distributors chose to publicize Kozintsev and Trauberg's film by positing its similarity to the very film against which it was reacting, *The Decembrists*.

S.V.D., or The Club of the Big Deed is noted for its striking visual style, which has sometimes been compared to that of Feuillade's famous French film *Fantomas*. Indeed, Shklovsky praised Kozintsev and Trauberg's film as the most elegant in Soviet cinema! In it, the actor Sergei Gerassimov plays the gambler and rogue Medok. In order to escape arrest, the crafty

Medok fabricates a tale about a ring which he wears. The ring bears the initials S.V.D., and Medok weaves a mystery around them. Thus the rogue claims that the initials identify him as a participant in the forthcoming Decembrist conspiracy against the tsar. Just as he would gamble on any game of chance, so Medok has chosen to gamble on the outcome of the political uprising. After the failure of the uprising, however, Medok's treachery is finally unmasked.

The subversion of the conventions of historical costume drama is achieved through the carnivalistic attitude of the eccentric style. The gambler—like the magician in *The Devil's Wheel*—is a characteristic type of the carnival world. The special ambiguity and ambivalence of the carnivalistic, as Bakhtin charts it, is implicit, perhaps, in the shifting patterns of the gambler's playing cards. Like the film which depicts him, Medok is essentially ludic in character; for him, history becomes a vast game of chance to be played at. *S.V.D., or the Club of the Big Deed* contests the illusion of transparence and naturalness to which the conventional historical costume film aspired.

If we situate the film in terms of the history of Soviet cinema in general, we will discover it to be quite different indeed from later approaches to the topic of Revolution in films of the 1930s. In *S.V.D., or The Club of the Big Deed*, the failure of the uprising is laid to its disdain of mass support. This failure is analyzed in terms of the fact that it is a coup, made by a handful of officers. Later, under Stalin, any hint that a spontaneous uprising of the masses might be a prerequisite of Revolution would be effaced. During the period of triumphant Stalinism, the official—and only—view of revolution was as a voluntarist affair.

In a sense, *S.V.D., or the Club of the Big Deed* was a preparation for Kozintsev and Trauberg's superb historical analysis in their 1929 film on the Paris Commune, *The New Babylon,* which is often regarded as the greatest work of the FEKS period. The 1871 uprising of the Paris Commune is scrutinized through the film's central metaphor of bourgeois decadence, an opulent department store called The New Babylon. The film's story is organized around the character of a young proletarian girl named Louise who is employed in the department store, and the essential structural tension of the film is that between proletariat and bourgeoisie. *The New Babylon* is indeed a stunning example of political cinema.

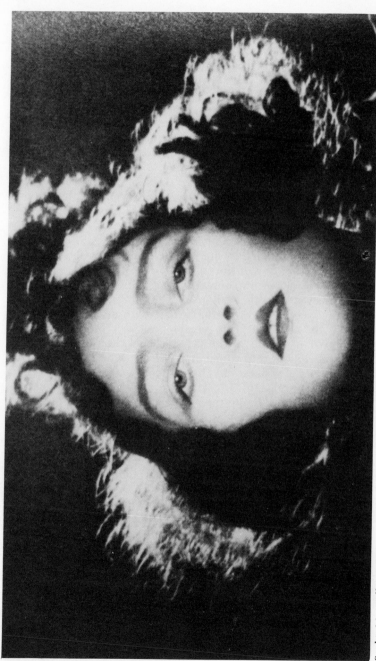

Sophie Magarill in *S.V.D.*

Kozintsev has recalled that, after the completion of *S.V.D., or The Club of the Big Deed,* he and Trauberg were summoned to Goskino in Moscow. There they were informed that it was deemed that their period of apprenticeship was now finished. In recognition of this, the two directors were called upon to undertake an important project, a film on the theme of the Paris Commune. Kozintsev and Trauberg did not hesitate for a moment, for this project was precisely the sort of thing they wanted to do. Research for the project would be undertaken in Paris. Thus, in February 1928, the directors set off for a three-week visit to the French capital. As Trauberg has noted, however, the scenario for the film was actually written before the trip to Paris. Evidently, then, the film was to be less a reproduction of reality than an exploration of a Paris of the imagination. This fact is significant indeed, for it suggests a fundamental impulse of the film.

The Parisian journey, however, was important for the film's visual style. In Paris the writer Ilya Ehrenburg guided Kozintsev and Trauberg about the city, so that they might assimilate as much of the atmosphere as possible in a short time. Excited by the sights and sounds of the urban scene, the filmmakers took numerous still photographs. It must be noted, though, that Kozintsev later pointed out that they had no intention of using these photographs for any attempt at realistic reproduction; rather, they hoped to use them to invoke associations once they had returned to the Soviet Union. Again, their emphasis was upon film's potential for poetic effects. *The New Babylon* was not to be a conventional historical drama; Kozintsev and Trauberg had already set forth a critique of this genre in *S.V.D., or The Club of the Big Deed.* It was their firm belief that art was not simply imitation, and it was this disdain for simple mimesis that determined the stylization of their filmic forms.

Part of Kozintsev and Trauberg's research in preparation for *The New Babylon* was intertextual in character. That is, the two filmmakers carefully studied art of the Commune period. Manet, Daumier, Degas, and Renoir were scrutinized for clues to the solution to the problem of visual style. Other intertextual research involved the study of relevant literary texts, Zola, for example. And a most important text considered in this regard was Marx's *The Class Struggle in France.* Kozintsev believed that it was their intensive scrutiny of this text which was the essential springboard for their own creative work. For Kozintsev and Trauberg, Marx's text conjured up an image of a "ghostly Paris," which proved to be essential to their conception of *The New Babylon*. Any consideration of Marx and art must take into account Kozintsev and Trauberg's creative reading of *The Class Struggle in France*.

As we might expect, it was difficult indeed to discover the precise filmic means for achieving the "ghostly" look suggested by Marx's text. The two filmmakers were rather disappointed by the early rushes, which struck them as not so different from the conventional costume films which they disdained. It seems that it was the cameraman, Andrei Moskvin, who solved the aesthetic problems posed by their desire for a "ghostly" look. For instance, a portrait lens was used which flattened the depth of space and softened the edges of the image. In addition, the placement of the actors on a platform shifted the relation between the static foreground and the dynamic action behind. Another tactic involved the use of lighting to manipulate the shadows of the foggy night views.[29]

The New Babylon is something of a landmark in the use of music in film, for it marks the first time that the composer Dmitri Shostakovitch wrote the score for a Kozintsev and Trauberg film. After the artistic success of their collaboration in this film, Shostakovitch would continue to work with Kozintsev and Trauberg. And, in later years, he would work with Kozintsev the solo director. The great uproar which greeted *The New Babylon* upon its release was also directed at Shostakovitch's score, which was highly innovative, to be sure. Kozintsev has pointed out the weakness of film music prior to Shostakovitch's work on *The New Babylon*. Previously, music operated to illustrate the visual image; on the contrary, Shostakovitch's approach was not to match sound and image, but to suggest a certain disjunction.

It may be said that *The New Babylon* remains today as exciting as it was in 1929. Indeed, in 1958, when Kozintsev viewed the film once more, in Belgium, his response was one of great excitement. His initial impulse was to talk to Trauberg and then to set out immediately to reedit it. The desire to reedit should not be taken as an indication of a disappointment with what he saw. On the contrary, it suggests that the film's material was still vitally alive for him. Jorge Luis Borges has described the distance felt when he encountered his own writings after they

The New Babylon.

Vsevelod Pudovkin in *The New Babylon*

were published. It seemed to Borges as if someone else had written them. In fact, he identified more with certain writings of other authors, such as Robert Louis Stevenson. This, then, was hardly Kozintsev's reaction in viewing *The New Babylon* so many years after its release. The artist's impulse here was to return to the work and continue to tinker with it. One other index of the film's continued potency ought to be mentioned here. In 1971, a proposal to screen *The New Babylon* on French television was rejected. The reason? The official explanation for the veto was that the 1929 film by the two young men was still "an incitement to revolt."[30]

The Transition to Sound

The New Babylon was the final silent film of Kozintsev and Trauberg. In 1931, with *Alone*, the two filmmakers made the transition to the sound cinema. But *Alone* also marks another kind of transition for Kozintsev and Trauberg, the shift to the aesthetic of Socialist Realism. Eccentrism and the *avant-garde* tactics of their FEKS period were to be displaced by the Socialist Realist approach. *Alone* may be taken as the bridge between the earlier work and the Maxim trilogy of the 1930s. What are some of the indications of this shift? For the first time, in *Alone*, Kozintsev and Trauberg moved away from the use of typage and the mass hero to a fuller exploration of the psychology of the individual hero. Indeed, the shift in the 1930s to the so-called "positive hero"—the voluntarist individual acting in and consciously shaping history—was to be a dominant characteristic of the Socialist Realist cinema. Thus, in *Alone*, we witness the first real attempt on the part of Kozintsev and Trauberg to shape a story largely around a central character's development. As in the later, more schematic productions of the Socialist Realist cinema, in *Alone* the positive hero is shown in the process of attaining political consciousness.

 Alone is the story of a young female teacher who is sent to work in a remote outpost of Siberia. Her alienation in this totally strange setting is exacerbated by her "selfish" personal concerns. She has had to leave her handsome fiancé behind in the city. The film, then, explores the processes by which her encounter with hardship in Siberia, where she nearly dies, finally enables her to subordinate her personal desires to the interests of the people.

Alone was shot silent, and music and sound were added later. In their first sound film, Kozintsev and Trauberg attempt to manipulate the relations between sound and visual image. The repetition of a song entitled "How Good Life Will Be" is an interesting case in point. Until the film's conclusion, the song's repetition is utilized to undermine or comment ironically upon the visual image it accompanies. Thus the song is heard for the first time in the section of the film which depicts the teacher and her fiancé, who are still together in Leningrad. There they dream of marriage and personal happiness. Of course, she does not yet know of the teaching assignment which will take her to Siberia. The song, therefore, possesses a certain irony. Later, when the film shifts to Siberia, we hear the song again. It accompanies the image of a selfish and ineffectual president of the local soviet and his wife. The couple is only interested in personal happiness; thus the music links them to the young girl and her fiancé. Both couples, it would seem, set personal happiness above the larger social good. Finally, at the film's conclusion, the song is encountered again. This time, sound and image do not collide. As the song is heard, the girl, whose life has been in danger, is shown being rescued by a plane sent by the people; she has been transformed into a truly social being. Sound and image combine to suggest "how good life will be."

In his essay "Socialist Realism in the Art of Cinema," the Soviet critic Semyon Freilikh seizes upon the importance of Kozintsev and Trauberg's *Alone*. Why *Alone?* For Freilikh, Soviet film history is "one of the appearance and consolidation of socialist realism in cinema art." In seizing upon *Alone,* Freilikh posits a fissure in Kozintsev and Trauberg's work. Thus he speaks of "the formalist period which we reject, and the 'realist' period which we accept, beginning with *Alone.*"[31] With *Alone,* then, a new phase is adumbrated; with *The Youth of Maxim,* it will be fully initiated. Freilikh, for whom this new phase is a welcomed shift, subscribes to a critical methodology determined by the aesthetic of Socialist Realism. Thus, at this point it will be necessary for us to consider in some detail the aesthetic of Socialist Realism as it evolved in the 1930s, and Kozintsev and Trauberg's relation to it.

3

Socialist Realism

AFTER THE TRANSITIONAL FILM *Alone,* Kozintsev and Trauberg set to work on what would be a trilogy of films, whose focus of interest was the development of a fellow named Maxim. This trilogy—consisting of *The Youth of Maxim, The Return of Maxim,* and *The Vyborg Side*—stands as a landmark of the cinema of Socialist Realism. This cinema is something of an unknown territory even within the realm of film scholarship. As we have seen, there is today enormous interest in the manifestations of the cinematic *avant-garde.* But the cinema of Socialist Realism is an entirely different case. There is, perhaps, even a desire to repress this cinema. After all, its inception marked the extinction of the *avant-garde;* and, in aesthetic terms, *Strike* is surely superior to *Alexander Nevsky!* Moreover, Socialist Realism is inevitably associated with triumphant Stalinism, an historical moment in which the Revolution was short-circuited. For students of the cinema, however, Socialist Realism must not be repressed. On the contrary, it needs to be subjected to a thorough scrutiny. In *Writing Degree Zero,* Roland Barthes has proposed that "a history of political modes of writing would . . . be the best of social phenomenologies."[1] In the same manner, the film student must undertake a scrutiny of the political modes of cinema. Barthes suggests the way in which form can operate as "an autonomous object, meant to signify a property which is collective and protective."[2] If we attend to the form of the Socialist Realist film, what, then, does it suggest more generally about the ideology of form? Because Socialist Realism is so unknown, so repressed, it is necessary, at this juncture in our analysis of Kozintsev, to consider the dominant aesthetic in the Soviet Union in the 1930s. Only then will we be able to

Pyotr Sobolevski and Yelenakuzina in Alone

Boris Chirkov in the title role of *The Youth of Maxim*

comprehend the position occupied by a film like *The Youth of Maxim* within the structure of Kozintsev's *oeuvre* as a whole. First the cinema of Socialist Realism must be situated intertextually in relation to the *avant-garde* cinema which preceded it.

In 1932 all of the diversified groups which had been struggling for control of the literary world were dissolved, for, henceforth, there was to be a single union for writers. Moreover, at that time, a single union undertook to represent all painters and sculptors. Now all of the Soviet arts began to move in a single direction; the *avant-garde* lingered on the horizon of the past, and the future suggested something quite different indeed. It was also in 1932 that the film *Counterplan,* directed by Friedrich Ermler, set the cinema on its new, unified track. In all of the arts, then, a single, obligatory aesthetic was set forth in the Soviet Union, Socialist Realism. It was, however, two years later, in 1934, that Socialist Realism was perhaps most forcefully initiated, at the First All-Union Congress of Soviet Writers. There the Russian author Maxim Gorky played a symbolic role and provided the new theory with what James Billington has characterized as a "measure of respectability."[3] In his famous speech at the Congress, Gorky moved to differentiate Socialist Realism from that Critical Realism which had been dominant in the previous century. For Gorky, Critical Realism "did not serve and cannot serve to educate socialist individuality, for in criticizing everything, it asserted nothing, or else, at the worst, reverted to an assertion of what it had itself repudiated."[4] The alienated, superfluous individual, who had occupied center-stage in European and Russian literature, was no longer to dominate in Socialist Realist art, for, according to Gorky, such personalities could not exist in the Soviet Union!

The transition from the *avant-garde* aesthetic of the 1920s to the Socialist Realist aesthetic of the 1930s involved a shift to mass culture. The famous difficulty of modernist art—as delineated, for instance, by José Ortega y Gasset in his essay "The Dehumanization of Art"—was subjected to the leveling process of mass culture. As Harold Rosenberg has pointed out, "the basis of mass culture in all its forms is an experience recognized as common to many people."[5] It might also be added that, with the Revolution over for all intents and purposes, an aesthetic of conflict simply posed too much of a threat to the powers that be. Indeed, Rosenberg has noted that " 'formal' art, in undermining accepted forms, has been a powerful agent in dissolving the social stereotypes maintained by them."[6] With the imposition of Socialist Realism, then, an aesthetic of conflict gives way to an aesthetic of stasis.

Obviously, the theory of Socialist Realism is prescriptive in character. Yet precisely what it prescribes has never quite been made clear. The offical codification of the theory proposes that it "requires from the artist a truthful, historically concrete representation of reality in its revolutionary development."[7] But what is a "truthful" representation? It has been argued by defenders of Socialist Realism that it is not as rigid a system as its critics make it out to be; indeed, the lack of formal prescription in the codified formula is stressed in this regard. It may also be suggested, however, that this ambiguity is not entirely innocent. Thus, Billington has evoked the "formula for keeping writers in a state of continuing uncertainty as to what it required of them: an invaluable device for humiliating the intellectuals by encouraging the debilitating phenomena of anticipatory self-censorship."[8] The insight may be extended to the other arts as well. Socialist Realism, with its ambiguous demands, involves tactics for keeping intellectuals in place. Indeed, the Socialist Realist artist would never know what was expected of his work; an explicit threat would ever hang above him. In this Kafkaesque situation, the artist could not know precisely what would elicit the wrath of those in a position to break him.

A Soviet Hollywood

In practice, in the cinema, Socialist Realism meant a return—heralded by Ermler's *Counterplan,* confirmed by the Vasilievs' *Chapayev* (1934), and officially endorsed in 1935 at the All Union Conference of Cinematographic Workers—to the illusionist discourse of linear narrative. That aesthetic of Realism, largely displaced by the *avant-garde* movement of the 1920s, was to make a triumphant return. Indeed, it was the declared aim of the head of the Soviet film industry, Boris Shumyatsky, to create a Soviet Hollywood! The implications of this desire are significant. The creation of a double of Hollywood may seem a strange ambition for a man representing the sworn enemies of capitalism; why desire to emulate these very capitalists' most successful creation? Yet it may be argued that the Soviet

Socialist Realist cinema, as it began to emerge in the 1930s, and
the classic Hollywood cinema shared much, not simply at the
level of content but, much more importantly, at the level of style
as meaning. Moreover, the Hollywood system, as the Soviets
perceived it, possessed, as a principal feature, an organization for
mass production. The Soviets discerned in the Hollywood system
something quite similar to what Barthes has described as the
"car system." In the "car system," Barthes has proposed, there is
a basic model variable only by the customer's choice of "color
and fittings."[9] One might say that both the Hollywood system
and its Soviet "double" instituted their own versions of the "car
system." First in Hollywood, and later in the Soviet Union under
the official aegis of Socialist Realism, film after film was turned
out from a basic model, each varying only in terms of what may
be metaphorically termed "color and fittings." The claim, of
course, may be made that the range of available variations was
wider in the case of Hollywood, that speech (*parole* there was
somewhat "richer," but this is not to deny that these variations,
like those in the Soviet system, remained on the level of "color
and fittings." Barthes has proposed a stylistic analysis concerned
with models, with ideological classification rather than with
individuations.[10] Such an approach is appropriate to an analysis of
Socialist Realist cinema in general, and of the Socialist Realist
films of Kozintsev and Trauberg in particular. Indeed, if *The
Youth of Maxim* seems aesthetically "richer" than most other
Socialist Realist films, it is largely a result of "color and fittings";
that is, the film conforms quite rigorously to the Socialist Realist
model.

In the Socialist Realist cinema, an aspiration toward harmony
displaces the conflict which marked the *avant-garde* cinema of
the 1920s. The Socialist Realist cinema strives for totality and
organicity. It is a transparent, "styleless" style which seeks to
mask its own making. The shift to Socialist Realism may be
understood in relation to Stalin's modification of the dialectical
laws; in particular, the elimination of the crucial law of the
negation of the negation effectively operated to bring the
dialectic to a halt. That is, the dialectic which posited movement
through conflict underwent a metamorphosis into a dialectic
which posited gradual growth and change, conflictless progress:
a dialectic which is, of course, quite undialectical. It is not
surprising, then, that, with the suspension of the law of the

negation of the negation, harmony became a goal of the Socialist Realist cinema. That harmony is embodied not only thematically, but formally as well. In theory, for the Soviets, the clashing forces of history had been stilled within their country. The nontranscendent status of art was, in effect, officially decreed. As Herbert Marcuse has written, "Soviet realism goes beyond artistic implementation of political norms by accepting the established social reality as the final framework for the artistic content, transcending it neither in style nor in substance. . . . The future is said to be nonantagonistic to the present."[11] Marcuse suggests that if the future is really nonantagonistic to the present, the transcendent function of art has been eliminated. The Revolution freezes. It is this frozen Revolution which is codified in the aesthetic of Socialist Realism.

Of all the major figures from the *avant-garde* period of the 1920s, none appeared to make the transition to Socialist Realism with more apparent success than Kozintsev and Trauberg. This success, however, was only transitory. After their first full-fledged Socialist Realist film, *The Youth of Maxim*, they increasingly found themselves unable to discover viable aesthetic solutions to the increasingly stringent constraints of Socialist Realism. In *The Youth of Maxim* elements lingering from the triumphant FEKS style may still be discerned. However, by the time of the third film of the trilogy, *The Vyborg Side*, such elements are few indeed. Kozintsev and Trauberg's situation improved briefly during the war, when the situation in the arts in general became more open; but in the immediate postwar years, during the period of the harsh attack on the arts by Stalin's cultural commissar Andrei Zhdanov, Kozintsev and Trauberg's *Simple People* was singled out for criticism and banned. The film was only released during the so-called "thaw," or de-Stalinization, in 1956.

Maxim

A scrutiny of *The Youth of Maxim* will suggest some of the ways in which Kozintsev and Trauberg attempted to conform to the demands of Socialist Realism while yet maintaining aesthetic interest. It seems, in fact, that *The Youth of Maxim* is the truly great success of a period that meant tragedy for Soviet cinema. Indeed, it may be the single film of triumphant Socialist Realism which can actually bear comparison with the great films of the silent period!

The Youth of Maxim is the first film in a trilogy tracing the rise of a young worker from unconscious victim to revolutionary activist and eventually to political commissar in the new state bank after the Bolshevik Revolution. In contrast to their films of the FEKS period, which stress conflict and disjunctures, *The Youth of Maxim* aspires to embody an ideology of totality. In contrast to the FEKS films, which are preoccupied with movements and gestures, *The Youth of Maxim* reveals a radical shift in interest to a scrutiny of faces. The interest has turned from rhythm to such concerns as theme and character, earlier disdained by Kozintsev and Trauberg. The FEKS films had been subjected to criticism in part because of what was deemed to be their excessive "aestheticism." The Soviet film critic Lebedev had argued that the FEKS works were inaccessible to the average filmgoer.[12] Hence, in the shift to Socialist Realism, Kozintsev and Trauberg moved to develop a style which aspires to transparence, which no longer calls attention to itself. The spectator's attention now is to be squarely focused on the characters, who are to be watched as if they were real people. That they are filmic images is to be repressed.

The ideology of totality which informs and shapes *The Youth of Maxim* is obviously consonant with the needs of Stalinist stabilization. Again and again in this film, it is coherence and order which triumph. This coherence and order reflect the spirit of the Stalinist state. The components of the medium are harnessed in the service of this desired coherence. For example, as the following scrutiny of the film will detail, sound is often utilized as a kind of "paste" which smoothes over breaks in the aesthetic object. Quite consonant with this ideology of totality is the elaboration of coherent, seemingly unbroken spaces from which conflict has been effaced. We witness as well the crucial shift of attention from bodily gesture and rhythm—which had been typical of the FEKS period—to the delineation of the individual hero's psychology via the play of expression upon the face.

The Youth of Maxim recalls the format of the *bildungsroman*, the novel of education and inner development. Quite simply, Kozintsev and Trauberg trace the education of the young Maxim. Maxim's formative years are charted by means of certain rigorously worked-out cinematic strategies. In a remarkable sense, Kozintsev and Trauberg have somehow managed to harness the possibilities of the medium to give a new twist to the *bildungsroman*. Significantly, Maxim's education is reflected in his facial expressions, upon which the camera focuses again and again.

It was Bela Balazs who underscored the cinematic preoccupation with the face of man. For Balazs, "facial expression is the most subjective manifestation of man, more subjective even than speech, for vocabulary and grammar are subject to more or less universally valid rules and conventions, while the play of features . . . is a manifestation not governed by objective canons, even though it is largely a matter of imitation."[13] According to Balazs, then, this subjectivity is objectivized in the cinematic device of the close-up. Thus, in their chronicle of Maxim's education and inner development, Kozintsev and Trauberg attend to the subtle play of emotions upon the face. We watch the young Maxim, played by Boris Chirkov, react to the world that surrounds him. It is as if the world can be seen making its mark upon Maxim's face. In this manner, Maxim's feelings are exteriorized, made concrete. Interiority is rendered legible upon the face of man.

Kozintsev and Trauberg enable the audience to read Maxim's face by so frequently placing those who speak to him beyond the sight of the camera in off-screen space. We can hear what they say; but, for large segments of time, we are unable to see them. Instead, we see Maxim. In one sequence of the film, Maxim is subjected to a series of laboratory tests before he is imprisoned. There is a sense in which throughout much of the film Maxim is the subject of a whole series of complex investigations. In conformity with the model of Socialist Realist film, Kozintsev and Trauberg focus their attention upon the scrutiny of the individual hero. The attention paid to the play of emotions upon Maxim's face is one of the ways in which Kozintsev and Trauberg manage to give the *bildungsroman* format a strong cinematic character.

Some examples of this strategy will be revealing here. Early in *The Youth of Maxim*, the lad is employed as an industrial worker in a plant whose conditions are evidently inhumane. Maxim is called in to the office of the rather ominous factory director. It seems that the factory director wishes to speak to Maxim about something. Thus, when Maxim comes to the office, we hear the factory director speak to him, but we do not at first see the source of that voice. Instead, the camera steadily inspects Maxim. This strategy, of course, tends to animate a certain amount of suspense and expectation. We do not yet know what it is that the factory director wants. This suspense is intensified by our not being permitted to see the factory director as he speaks.

Our scrutiny is limited to Maxim alone. We have no choice but to examine his face so as to gauge his response to the factory director's words. At first, Maxim does not know what it is that the factory director wants to talk to him about. Until now Maxim has played the fool; he does not care much about anything except the circus, women, and his buddies. As the factory director talks to him, Maxim continues to act in a lighthearted, totally unserious manner. But when the factory director reveals his purpose— when he tells Maxim what it is that he wants of him—we are able to observe a pronounced change upon the lad's face. We learn that the factory director is deeply concerned about revolutionary propaganda that has been spread to the employees in the factory. He wants to put a stop to this situation. But first he must be able to determine the source of this propaganda. So he asks Maxim to spy on his fellow workers. Perhaps Maxim can locate the source of this subversive propaganda. Maxim's antic pose drops away. His changed mood is exteriorized; the subjective is rendered objective. His response to the factory director's request is rendered legibly upon his face. The fool's smile turns into something quite different indeed. This crucial metamorphosis is recorded for us by the camera.

A similar device to this one is utilized at other junctures in *The Youth of Maxim*. Thus, after he participates in a worker's riot, Maxim is sent to jail. There he meets the Bolshevik Polivanov, whom the audience has already encountered earlier in the film's prologue. Title cards punctuate the film throughout, dividing it into sections which provide the work with its overall structure. Now a title card tells us that Maxim is to enter the university. Of course, this statement is highly ironic. There is a disparity between it and that which is actually transpiring. Indeed, the prison is to be Maxim's university! Here is where Maxim's higher education will really begin. It is his meeting here with the remarkable Polivanov, which is to prove crucial to his formation. Polivanov warmly inquires about what Maxim likes to read. This question also possesses its irony within the context of the film, for the factory director had also inquired as to Maxim's reading habits. The factory owner wanted to know whether or not Maxim was interested in subversive literature. Instead, he discovered that Maxim had been spending his time reading cheap popular fiction: specifically, *Anton Krechet, the Bandit.* Now, when Polivanov inquires about Maxim's reading habits, he is almost certainly hoping to hear that the lad has looked at that same subversive literature feared by the factory director. When Maxim replies to the question, his face indicates that his attitude toward things has changed substantially. Indeed, there is a note of irony discernible in his face as he pronounces the name of the book: *Anton Krechet, The Bandit.* Now he knows the score a bit. He has developed a certain animosity toward the ruling class. His mocking smile demands to be read for the irony it communicates. Next, we listen as Polivanov tells Maxim of those prisoners who are to be executed in a short time. Thus, the mocking smile turns to something quite different. The play of expression upon the face becomes a kind of shorthand. The list of those to be executed appears to inscribe itself upon Maxim's physiognomy; his response is exteriorized.

Later, after some turmoil in the prison, Maxim and Polivanov are punished by being confined to a small, dingy space. It is after Maxim's friend has been executed, and, naturally, he is bitter indeed. Maxim does not fear death; he merely seeks revenge. From off-screen space come Polivanov's words. In keeping with the importance of optimistic tragedy in Socialist Realism, Polivanov refuses to despair. He says that he intends to marry and send his grandchildren to a Socialist university. As we hear him tell of his faith in the outcome of the struggle, as we listen to his vigorous words of courage, we watch Maxim's face. This—we recall—is Maxim's university! Polivanov strenuously discourages thoughts of death. His words point to the necessary work that must be done. And there is an important role for Maxim in that work. The question arises: Will he join in the struggle? Again, we witness the play of expressions upon the lad's face. Polivanov's words have had their effect upon him, and that effect is clearly registered upon his physiognomy.

Later, when Maxim is about to be discharged from prison, the prison director's voice can be heard as Maxim stands before his desk; but for a time we see only Maxim's face. The source of that voice remains beyond the vision of the camera in off-screen space. The prison director, whom we do eventually glimpse, begins a recitation of the places from which Maxim has been banned. When he is released from prison, he will not be able to live in any of these places. The list includes virtually every possible place that Maxim might wish to go to. We watch Maxim's face as he listens to this absurdly long list. Maxim is located in the frame beneath a small portrait of the tsar. The contrast between the two men injects the sequence with further irony. Generally in the film—with few exceptions—the sound is naturalistic. That is, it emanates from someone or something we know to be on the scene at the moment, even if the camera cannot see it. One exception to this naturalistic use of sound is to be discovered in the present sequence. The director of the prison can still be heard reading from his ludicrously long list of forbidden locales, when we see the lad, no longer sitting in the prison director's office but leaving the prison through its doors. If we think about it for a moment, we will realize that by the time Maxim has left the prison the director has surely finished actually reading the list. But we continue to hear him reading it as we see an image of Maxim departing through the prison doors. This is one of the few times in *The Youth of Maxim* when the sound may be said to be somewhat divergent from the naturalistic norm. The filmmakers employ this use of nonnaturalistic sound here to exacerbate the sense of absurdity. The length of the prison director's list might well be characterized as Kafkaesque, for the lad has been banned from virtually everywhere.

Upon his release from prison, Maxim immediately observes his friend Natasha. Natasha is courting a bourgeois gentleman at the moment, so she finds it necessary to spurn Maxim's greetings. His puzzled expression is a masterful touch that indicates that the lad still has much to learn about the rather devious ways of the revolutionary struggle. Here, he cannot quite figure out what is going on. His education, of course, is far from complete!

Soon, at a rally in the countryside, Polivanov reads a letter from Lenin. Again, we do not watch Polivanov, but, rather, Maxim's face as he imbibes the words of the great revolutionary. The tsarist police manage to discover the location of this illegal rally. Maxim escapes and flees through the labyrinthine wilderness. Maxim's face can be seen to emerge from some bushes. We hear some unidentifiable noises, which seem rather scratchy. In addition, some ghastly laughter can be made out. But at first—if only for a moment—we do not see the source of these threatening and ambiguous sounds. Their ambiguity underscores the ambiguity of Maxim's position. We know that something is wrong from the peculiar character of these sounds, as well as from the look written upon Maxim's face, which appears troubled as he emerges from the bushes. Here, of course, Kozintsev and Trauberg aim at building a certain suspense. What is the source of these scratchy sounds? This is the question that we ask for the instant when we can see only Maxim's face. Now we are permitted to see the mysterious source of these sounds. It is a gramophone played for the entertainment of a bourgeois family on an outing. At the sight of Maxim, the pompous bourgeois father howls for the help of the police. Maxim flees into the bushes once more. We see him hurtling through the wilderness at top speed. Moreover, as we watch his flight, we continue to hear the same ghastly sounds of the gramophone. The laughter is made to appear to be pursuing him. The threat implicit in his flight is underscored by the shrewd use of this ominous sound; its source in the bourgeois family's gramophone, moreover, assumes a certain political significance.

Here, then, is another significant instance in the film in which the focus on Maxim's physiognomy is coupled with an auditory experience that leaves the audience momentarily puzzled as to its source. After a lapse of time on the run, Maxim makes his way to an apartment occupied by Natasha. Upon his arrival she greets him at the door, and we can tell that he sees something behind her in the apartment. Bela Balazs has proposed the manner in which the sound film might educate our ears, just as the silent cinema had sought to educate our eyes. In this sequence in the film, then, we hear a strange sound which we cannot identify. We know that its source—whatever it might be—has an unsettling effect on the newly arrived Maxim, for we can read his response upon his face. But we are unable to determine—if only momentarily—the source of the sound we hear. Its source is the object of Maxim's stare, but that stare passes into off-screen space, beyond our own view. This momentary lack of knowledge is quite frustrating. At last, though, the camera tells us what we want to know. In a brief moment, anticipation has been built. We discover that the source of the sound is a tsarist officer slurping inelegantly from a glass. One question is immediately replaced by another; now that we know the source of this strange sound, we want to know precisely what the big fellow is doing in Natasha's apartment. Just as one mystery is solved, another unfolds. Of course, the first mystery should not have been so puzzling; after all, we have so often heard people slurping liquids from a glass. Why, then, could we not identify this sound? Balazs's ideas about the education of the ear are quite relevant here. Kozintsev and Trauberg manage to educate our ears in this sequence. Indeed, we will never forget the sound of liquid slurped inelegantly from a glass!

The sequences scrutinized thus far suggest Kozintsev and Trauberg's shrewd manipulation of off-screen space. In this regard, the film's opening sequence is of great interest. The New Year celebration recorded in this sequence begins with a black screen. We see nothing. Voices, whose sources we are unable to see, proclaim New Year greetings. Next the eye is assaulted by a New Year celebration stamped by the radical mark of FEKS. The camera moves furiously, as carousing celebrants pass quickly before our vision. The contrast between the black screen with which the sequence opens and the orgy of images that follows is striking indeed. Within the context of the film's overall structure, even more striking is the contrast between this moment of dissonant style with the rest of the film.

Polivanov comes upon a hallway with two different apartment doors visible. One door opens to let in some ecstatic celebrants. Smoke, noise, and music gush forth from the open doorway as the celebrants enter. Polivanov is visibly engulfed in the smoke, which represents a locale we cannot really see, because it remains beyond the camera's view. When the celebrants have entered, the door closes. Behind Polivanov is a window through which we watch a shadow show of the madcap party within. Polivanov's business takes him to the other door. Within the apartment of his Bolshevik comrades, Polivanov dictates a letter to the workers. For Polivanov and his comrades, then, the New Year assumes a political significance. The noises of the celebration in the adjoining apartment counterpoint the activity of the Bolsheviks. As the Bolsheviks engage in their serious business, they move in an ambience penetrated by the sounds of the mindless celebrations beyond the camera's view. The effect is rather unsettling. Bela Balazs has noted that "all sound has an identifiable place in space. . . . This possibility of placing sound also helps to hold together shots the action of which takes place in the same space."[14] Here, then, the two apartments are located in the same building. Hence, the noise from one filters into the other. We get a sense of a single structure.

Outside, Polivanov can still hear the sounds of the party. At a distance, that sound disappears. It is followed by the silence of the night. This silence is punctuated by a police whistle which signals a raid on the Bolshevik hideout. In a sense, the sound of the police whistle defines the silence of the night. In turn, it is only the silence that permits us to hear the whistle as vividly as we do. Polivanov flees. He ducks into a hallway and shuts the doors behind him. Through their frames we watch crowds passing by on the street. Within the hallway, Polivanov meets an old Menshevik friend. Strains of Chopin can be heard from afar. The two men enter a room that is cluttered with clothing. We know by all this clothing that many people are in attendance. Also, we hear the music in full force. But the music and the people remain beyond the view of the camera. Indeed, even when the camera reveals the entire room, we do not yet see the source of the music. Instead, a single man emerges from behind the beaded curtains. We suspect that these beaded curtains lead to a room where all the people are: the source of the music. Still, the source of the predominant sounds lingers in off-screen space. Eventually, cavorting New Year celebrants do in fact emerge from behind the beaded curtains. We see people dancing and singing. A certain distance develops between the Bolshevik and the celebrants. They remain securely behind the beaded curtains. The host is himself a Menshevik, a member of an alternate wing of the revolutionary group; and this distance underscores that other distance—between Bolshevik and Menshevik.

The sequence involving the funeral procession of a worker killed in an accident also makes use of off-screen space in a particularly shrewd manner. Kozintsev and Trauberg here manage to valorize the funeral procession by keeping it in off-screen space for some time. Instead of seeing the funeral procession itself, we see the reactions of the people in the street as it passes by. We hear the singing of those engaged in the procession. But, for some time, we are not permitted to see them. Instead, we are restricted to the physiognomies of the crowd. That which every face in the crowd seems to be turned toward is valorized. Finally, we are permitted to see the funeral procession. Had we seen it all along it would not carry the same powerful charge that it does now. Maxim himself is a member of that procession. In a striking shot, Kozintsev and Trauberg isolate Maxim's physiognomy before the passing procession. His own face is lighted prominently, and we witness the subtle passage of emotions upon it. Deciding to join the procession, and disappearing into its surge, Maxim passes off-screen with the other workers. Cinematic means are utilized to convey a sense of solidarity. Now, the continuing procession, the lengthy flow of workers, fills the screen.

Coherent Spaces

In the cinema of illusionism—as opposed to the cinema of the *avant-garde*—space must above all be coherent. Thus, for instance, Kozintsev and Trauberg utilize cinematic means to create the coherent space of the prison in which Maxim is incarcerated after the workers' riot. At first, we view him alone in his cell, as he talks to himself. Then the camera explores the locale: the door, the window. Even though Maxim is no longer in sight, we continue to hear his voice, whose source is in off-screen space. That voice unifies the successive shots. The space beyond our sight is represented, moreover, by the voice of the prison guard, who tells Maxim to stop singing. His voice suggests the space beyond the cell. The prison guard is made particularly ominous by the device of not permitting us to view him as he issues his command.

Kozintsev and Trauberg manage to unify successive shots of locales within the prison by means of sound. We deduce a sense of the prison as a single space. Significantly, formal means are appropriated to provide the prisoners in different cells with solidarity. A crucial point in the depiction of Maxim's stay in the prison is the execution of a group of prisoners. Among them is Maxim's dear friend, Dyoma. We see a woman furiously weeping in her cell. Kozintsev and Trauberg link this woman's plight to the others in the prison in the following way: even when we cut to the cell in which Maxim and Polivanov are incarcerated, we still hear the feverish cries. A complex of emotions is inscribed upon Polivanov's face. At this point, we do not see the source of the sound; we know that it is the poor woman languishing in another cell. Polivanov is quite powerless to help. He hears her cries as we do, but just as she remains off-screen for us, so for Polivanov this despairing comrade is out of reach. Polivanov and Maxim begin now to sing. Their singing is a clever device to provide the prisoners with solidarity. We watch the woman in her small cell as she hears her comrades' voices in song. She too begins to sing this song of unity. Prisoners in all the cells of the prison thus join in. The divergent spaces of the prison have been rendered as one—the aesthetic of totality adhered to.

The prison guards are sent in now to muffle the heroic song of the comrades. We see these powerful guards as they attempt to quiet the singing prisoners. Kozintsev and Trauberg here devise a masterful strategy. We do not at first hear the sounds of the struggle between the prisoners and the guards. Instead, we continue to hear the heroic singing of the comrades even though a given shot may picture an individual prisoner being subdued by the guards; the sound of the struggle is not recorded. Hence, the apparent defeat is erased. The song continues in spite of individual defeats! Kozintsev and Trauberg thus fashion a clever formal device which makes the requisite ideological point. In another major Socialist Realist film of the period, Yefim Dzigan's *We From Kronstadt* (1936), a commisar proclaims that where one Red falls thousands will rise to take his place. The sound of the triumphant singing is what we hear in this sequence of Kozintsev and Trauberg's film; the sounds of individual defeats are not recorded. Finally, we switch to naturalistic sound, as we hear individual prisoners being muffled by the guards. And yet, albeit with difficulty, they attempt to continue to sing the song of the workers. All in all, it is an especially potent sequence.

Sound is utilized as a tactic for achieving coherent space in another important sequence in the film, wherein Maxim participates in leading comrades to a secluded outdoor meeting in the wilderness led by Polivanov. Maxim's job is to play the guitar at the side of a lake and give directions to the approaching comrades. His music leads the comrades to the spot where he appears to lounge innocently. As comrades approach, his singing defines the space in the wilderness with which the camera is concerned. As comrades proceed beyond Maxim to the next sentry, a man who appears to be fishing for pleasure, still we hear Maxim's song which unifies the space. Later, as Polivanov dramatically reads a letter from Lenin, we watch Maxim's face at the edge of the meeting. The officials have been tipped off as to the location of the illegal gathering. They manage to accost the fisherman sentry who has remained at his post on the lookout. But we do not hear the sounds of the struggle. Instead, it is the words of Lenin as recited by Polivanov that we hear.

We know silence only by means of the sound which punctuates and defines it for us. The manner in which sounds punctuate silence is considered at various junctures in Kozintsev and Trauberg's film. We have already considered the manner in which police whistles punctuate the silent night in the film's prologue. Throughout the film, the whistles of the factory punctuate the space of the action which is thus defined in relation to the struggle of the workers. In a particularly tense scene in which Natasha is almost arrested for subversive activities by the tsarist police, the suspenseful quiet in the room is punctuated by the enormous officer who rather inelegantly blows his nose. As one of the workers is ejected from the room so that Natasha can be interrogated he lets his accordion unfold. The noise created by this unfolding punctuates the tense silence that came before the interrogation. Later, the accordion is used again to punctuate the silence. Just before the riot of the workers at the scene of the funeral procession for the man who has been killed in the factory, there is a suspenseful, painfully tense stand-off between the workers and the police. The police have ordered the workers to halt the procession. The body of the dead worker will be escorted to the hospital by the police. But the workers refuse to disperse. They stand firm in their resistance. Dyoma and some buddies, depressed at the death of their friend, Andrei, have spent some time in a local establishment getting drunk. This establishment happens to be located precisely where the tense stand-off between the police and the workers is transpiring. Dyoma and his buddies, roaring drunk, emerge into the light of day. They sing and carouse in drunken fashion. Moreover, they play the accordion. These sounds, then, serve to punctuate the silence of the tense stand-off. Dyoma's path has been one of escape. The workers who have engaged the tsarist police have taken direct action. How deeply out of place is the escapist's route is made clear in this startling use of sound: Dyoma's drunken songs are ludicrously alien to the serious confrontation taking place.

Initiation and Expectation

The Youth of Maxim traces a young man's initiation. In mythical terms, the death of the lad's friend Andrei in a factory accident results in one stage of Maxim's rebirth. The death by execution of another friend, Dyoma, signals yet another stage of Maxim's rebirth. Thus, Maxim is initiated into political consciousness. It can be argued that the thematic of initiation fits quite neatly into the narrative form of the film. Writing about the kind of linear narrative, which, we have suggested, *The Youth of Maxim* embodies, Barthes has written of its similarity to rites of initiation: "a long path marked with pitfalls, obscurities, stops, suddenly comes into light."[15] Such narratives, Barthes proposes, place truth at the end of expectation. Thus, it might be said that in *The Youth of Maxim*, the ultimate expectation is political consciousness. If, as Barthes argues, such narratives move toward order, Polivanov's intention to marry and send his children to a socialist university looks ahead toward the order at the end of the road.

In this scrutiny of *The Youth of Maxim*, we have noted some ways in which Kozintsev and Trauberg manage to create coherent spaces by cinematic means. We have emphasized the particularly shrewd manner in which the filmmakers utilize sound to link successive shots, to posit an image of solidarity. Indeed, as Barthes has demonstrated, the closed or "readerly" text is governed by what he calls a "law of solidarity."[16] Here, then, the dissonance of the FEKS period is largely smoothed away. Yet, as we have seen, it lingers in the exuberant opening of the film with its furiously moving camera. In those moments, so reminiscent of the tactics of the FEKS period, we are frequently disoriented. That dissonance, that disorientation, drops away in the rest of the film, which evinces—by and large—that "law of solidarity" to which Barthes refers. Rejecting the radical tactics of FEKS, the film's successive shots are *linked*, frequently by means of sound; the notion of montage as collision is largely repressed. Thoroughly coherent spaces unfold. An ideology of totality is the film's underlying informing principle, as it is in the Socialist Realist cinema in general.

Significantly, Barthes links the closed or "readerly" text to an historical aspiration: "By participating in the need to set forth the end of every action (conclusion, interruption, closure, denouement), the readerly declares itself to be historical."[17] And, indeed, the events depicted in Kozintsev and Trauberg's *The Youth of Maxim* clearly locate themselves historically. This declaration takes a most obvious form; the film begins with a shot of a history book—Professor Pokrovsky's *History of Russia*. First, the book is seen closed. Then, quite suddenly, it begins to open— *by itself*. No hand emerges to turn the pages! The self-consciousness and reflexivity of the *avant-garde* is gone. Instead, the events that unfold in *The Youth of Maxim* are situated in an historical tense. Its action is given a certain pastness. It is closed—inscribed within the pages of what Emile Benveniste has called historical narrative. Notably, the book seems to open by itself; these events are posited as the true past. No human hand is needed to turn the pages of history. This, then, is the confidence game of historical narrative, the assumption that there is a single history, a single truth, that may be rendered in transparent fashion. Locating the action of the film within the closed past of historical narrative guarantees its coherence. The shot of the history book is a significant adumbration of the structure of the film as a whole. We are told that this is not just the story of one man. There are many Maxims. One stands for the many. In spite of his apparent individuations, Maxim is, in essence, mass man. This portrait would be sustained through the two other films of the trilogy in which Maxim's story is continued. At last, in *The Vyborg Side*, we find ourselves in the period after the Revolution. Maxim and Natasha assume responsible positions in the new state.

The Consolidation of Socialist Realism

By 1940 the Soviets had established an efficient filmic aesthetic consonant with the needs of the Stalinist state. By then, even the great masters of the *avant-garde* period—such as Kozintsev and Trauberg, Eisenstein, and Dovzhenko—had more or less learned—at enormous cost—how to make films that would operate within the constraints of Socialist Realism. For these filmmakers, of course, the task of conforming to the Socialist Realist aesthetic was not a simple procedure. We can see that the demands of the Socialist Realist model favored the rise of far less original filmmakers in the 1930s than in the golden age of the revolutionary cinema of the 1920s. Filmmakers like the Vasilievs fit into the mold far more precisely because of their lack of truly first-rate cinematic talent. Thus, if we trace the evolution of Socialist Realist cinema in the 1930s, we will note the rise of this kind of less distinctive director and the increasing difficulties faced by the great names of the 1920s, as they attempt to adapt to the shifting aesthetic style.

Moving through the years of the 1930s, we note the evolution and consolidation of the Socialist Realist model. We can trace the gradual sealing-off of openings for originality. In 1931, for example, there are films like Kozintsev and Trauberg's *Alone* and Dovzhenko's *Ivan*—both very much transitional films, still not entirely broken from the style of the 1920s. Or, even in 1933, it is obvious that the constraints of the model have not been irrevocably imposed, if we look at sadly neglected films like Boris Barnet's *Okraina* or Kuleshov's *The Great Consoler*. Both of these are every bit as interesting aesthetically as the films of the silent period, which are better known in this country. The complex structure of the Kuleshov film or the brilliant use of music and movement in the Barnet work mark authentic cinematic voices. After 1934, however, the model exerts increasingly strong pressure for conformity to its constraints. For example, most of the moments in Ermler's *Peasants*, which seem particularly strong in cinematic terms, are by that time possible only because he paid for such sequences with the obligatory Stalin sequence—in this case, a dream of Stalin. After this, there is very little deviation from the model possible. Even for the best filmmakers it became increasingly difficult to manage an authentic cinematic voice within those constraints embodied in the Socialist Realist aesthetic. The aesthetic of conflict has given way to the all-engulfing totality of Socialist Realism. The lifeless model could be stamped out again and again on the assembly line, producing numerous undistinguished films. Romm's *Lenin in October* (1937) is the model at its dismal height, the model with no original touches added, Socialist Realism pure and unadulterated. The model films of Socialist Realism—here, of course, *Chapayev* must come to mind—aspire to a condition in which the plane of the signifier, the marks of production, are masked. When the Socialist Realist ideal is realized, style becomes transparent, hence natural. All attention is to be focused on the film's content. It is to be as if one were looking directly at reality, not a mediated image.

If we look at Eisenstein's *Alexander Nevsky,* we discover that even here the old master of the *avant-garde* never achieved the transparency of filmmakers like the Vasilievs or Romm. If Eisenstein shifts here from a concern with montage, it is to a concern with composition. If we look at a film like Kozintsev and Trauberg's *The Vyborg Side,* we can see that in comparison even to the first film of the Maxim trilogy, the attention focused on the level of style, the opportunities for aesthetic pleasure—even if on the level of "color and fittings"—have been severely limited. By 1939, then, we may say that even the old masters of the Soviet *avant-garde* cinema have largely been tamed—for the moment at least. At this point, the model of Socialist Realism held monolithic sway over the Soviet cinema.

Simple People (1945)

During the war, much of the film industry was moved far from the center of political power to the outreaches of the republic. For a number of reasons—not the least of which was simple expediency—the wartime cinema underwent a considerable liberalization. The controls, which had been rigidly in place by the late 1930s, were relaxed somewhat. But in 1945 the war ended, and with it, almost immediately, appeared the first signs of an even more intensive effort at cultural regulation. All of the major arts were clearly warned, in a series of individual resolutions, that they must conform to stringent political demands. On September 4, 1946, the Central Committee of the Communist party issued a resolution, entitled "On the Moving Picture *Great Life,"* which was addressed to the cinema. It focused its attack on Leonid Lukov's film *Great Life,* but also condemned the latest films of Eisenstein, Pudovkin, and Kozintsev and Trauberg.

In the case of Kozintsev and Trauberg, the work in question was *Simple People,* a film which was completed in 1945. It was the first film to come out of the Lenifilm Studios after the severe war damage there. The story of *Simple People* involved a group of airplane workers evacuated during the war. In the attack, the reasons for the official condemnation were not given specifically.

But all four works which were included in the resolution by name—*Ivan the Terrible*, Part II, *Admiral Nakhimov*, *Great Life*, and *Simple People*—were branded "false and mistaken films." The resolution offered this explanation as to why some of the masters of the Soviet cinema had suddenly now made such erroneous productions: "many masters of cinematography, producers, directors, scenario writers, take their obligations thoughtlessly and irresponsibly and work dishonestly in the creation of moving pictures. Their chief mistake is their failure to study the business which they undertake." In other words, the films in question failed to conform to the political line of the moment. Anything which deviated in the slightest from an unequivocal singleness of meaning was now to be condemned by the powers that be.

The Council of Art of the Ministry of Cinematography, which had approved these now branded films was accused of the Stalinist transgression of "political neutrality." In addition, the accusation was made that personal friendships had been taken into consideration in the decision-making process. Thus the film industry was condemned in general for the "family atmosphere prevailing among creative workers in the field."[18] The resolution concluded by stating that the film industry was to reform itself, or else these workers might find that they might "pass out of circulation."

As a result of the Central Committee's resolution, all four films in question were banned. Kozintsev and Trauberg's longtime collaboration drew to an end.

Chirkov with Valentina Kibardina in *The Vyborg Side*

4

Don Quixote

IN MARCH 1953, Stalin died. Even before his death was officially announced to the public, jockeying for power had begun in the Soviet Union. The situation was unclear for a time, but eventually Nikita Khrushchev consolidated his power over his rivals and emerged as the dominant figure in Soviet politics. At the time of Stalin's death, both Soviet society and its culture were in a dreadful state. The once vanguard Soviet cinema was now suffering from the effects of more than two decades of unpredictable and all-pervasive censorship. The number of films produced had diminished drastically. In 1952, the year before Stalin's death, only five feature films were released. This small number is absolutely unbelievable in a nation the size of Russia, with a highly sophisticated tradition of film production. In years past, filmmakers around the world had looked to the Soviet cinema for leadership in the realms of film theory and practice. By now, however, it had become nearly impossible to get script approval in the Soviet Union. And, even if script approval were obtained against all odds, a project faced the impossible task of proceeding through a Kafkaesque system of checks at every stage of production. Indeed, by the time of Stalin's death, the Soviet film industry had no room for anything that held the faintest hint of aesthetic innovation or originality.

After all, the absolute insistence on that glossy, conflictless optimism which characterized the Socialist Realist cinema of triumphant Stalinism had virtually destroyed the once glorious Soviet cinema. Eisenstein had died in 1948, leaving the second part of his final brilliant work *Ivan the Terrible* banned, and the third part unfinished. Dovzhenko was tormented at every turn, but dared at one point to observe in his diary: "In this inertia of

77

Yuri Tolubeyev as Sancho Panza in Don Quixote

suspicion and degradation one can lose not just one's talent, but one's sanity and desire to go on living."[1] Pudovkin was apparently no longer distinguishable from any of the other Socialist Realist hacks. Kozintsev's longtime collaborator Trauberg had been a victim of the vicious campaign against the so-called "cosmopolitans" in 1949. Konstantin Simonov characterized cosmopolitanism as "the desire to undermine the roots of national pride because people without roots are easier to defeat and sell into the slavery of American imperialism." Thus, the journal *Iskusstvo Kino* located Trauberg as a member of a "group of aesthetician-cosmopolitans in cinema." Kozintsev found himself attacked implicitly for critical writing on the cinema which he had undertaken.[2] After the split with Trauberg, Kozintsev was to make two of the many biographies of historical figures which were characteristic of the late years of Stalinism. In 1947 he made *Pirogov,* which was the story of a nineteenth-century Russian surgeon. And in 1951 Kozintsev directed a filmic biography of Belinsky, the nineteenth-century radical critic.

Antonin and Mira Liehm have pointed out that, in 1952, even before the death of Stalin, there were some indications that the controls of cinema needed to be loosened somewhat. After his death, then, indications of liberalization gradually increased. Finally, in February 1956, Khrushchev shocked his listeners at the Twentieth Congress of the Soviet Communist party when he made the now famous "Secret Speech." In this speech, which did not remain secret for long, Khrushchev actually denounced the crimes of Stalin and attacked what he called Stalin's "cult of personality." Indeed, the effect of this important speech was absolutely electrifying. Its effect was quite strongly felt in the Soviet culture in general. The whole period of liberalization has come to be known by the title of a novel by Ilya Ehrenburg—the first part of which was published in 1954— *The Thaw.* The effect of the liberalization on almost every level of Soviet society was indeed like that of a thaw—as if the ice which had long frozen the people and their culture was now melting.

Gradually, changes took place in the Soviet cinema. The effect of the thaw upon this realm of aesthetic enterprise was felt both in the introduction of new themes—ones which had been forbidden in the years of triumphant Stalinism—and in formal innovations. Of course, it should be carefully noted that Socialist Realism itself was never renounced as the official aesthetic. But, as the Liehms point out, "it was not the negation of Socialist Realism but rather its most flexible interpretation that became the order of the day."[3] The limits of Socialist Realism were extended. For the first time in years, those utterly schematic films which had been typical of Soviet production in the late 1930s and the 1940s began to give way to films which could treat themes that had previously been prohibited. Moreover, stylistic originality became a factor once again in the Soviet cinema.

But the path to liberalization did not go so far as many had hoped. In 1956, the "events" in Poland, as well as the full-scale revolt in Hungary, were quickly to be followed by a tightening in the Soviet Union itself. After this, the pattern of liberalization and tightening in Soviet society has been a complex affair, responding to a number of factors. The cinema has been directly influenced by this pattern. The Liehms point out that it was precisely because the Soviets did perceive the importance of the cinema that they worked so carefully to control it.[4]

Throughout the uncertain years which followed the death of Stalin—years in which the situation for filmmakers was usually somewhat freer than it had been during his rule—Kozintsev was to occupy a significant position. He was to make films in the last years of his life which not only spoke of the situation in which he found himself, but which constituted very real challenges to the moribund aspects of Socialist Realism.

In 1957 Kozintsev initiated a pattern which was to mark the last phase of his career. In turning with vigor to the project of adapting great literary classics to the screen, Kozintsev triumphantly managed to escape the potentially ossifying effects of the sacred "classic" work. Adaptations of literary classics can be dull affairs indeed, thoroughly lacking in cinematic interest. In undertaking the task of adaptation, Kozintsev, however, was not merely retreating into the museum of the past. Instead, as an artist, he seized upon the past in order to illuminate the present. In these last films, the theoretical influence of Russian Formalism may be detected. After all, texts of the past are indeed "made strange" in Kozintsev's films of this final phase. Russian Formalism, moreover, stressed the manner in which art alludes to art. Works of art themselves, Kozintsev's final films may be taken to be "about" other works of art. The world is interpreted, then, through these classic texts, *Don Quixote, Hamlet,* and *King Lear.*

Inner Shocks

Kozintsev has remarked that "an artist is always like a
seismograph, recording the inner shocks of his epoch."[5] Indeed,
the *avant-garde* FEKS films of the 1920s had quite faithfully
recorded the signs of the early years of the Revolution. Their
aesthetic of conflict managed to suggest the spirit of the age. And
in the 1930s and the 1940s, Kozintsev and Trauberg's films again
provide a useful means for comprehending aspects of the shifting
times in which they were made. And again, after the death of
Stalin, the inner shocks of the self-revaluation of the Soviets
mark the films of Kozintsev's final phase.

In 1957, Kozintsev's cinematic adaptation of Cervantes's a
great novel *Don Quixote* was released. The film constitutes a
brilliant experiment in solving the aesthetic problems posed by
the cinematic adaptation of literary materials. Cervantes's
delightful novelistic creation is a man so immersed in books—
specifically in the literature of chivalry—that he sets out on a
parodic quest accompanied by the faithful Sancho Panza. In the
film, Don Quixote is quite brilliantly played by the great Soviet
actor Nikolai Cherkasov, who is especially well-known today for
his performance in Eisenstein's *Ivan the Terrible.* Don Quixote's
quest is, in essence, for social justice. He believes that it is his
duty to protect the downtrodden, the exploited, wherever he
may find them—and even when he imagines he finds them.
Riding on a skinny horse and wearing an ancient suit of armor and
a tin plate on his head, Don Quixote wields a giant lance as he
proceeds along his path. The image is, of course, cut through
with irony. Behind him, the short, ludicrously obese Sancho
Panza follows on his donkey, which he claims to have selected
because it is so close to the ground. Together, Don Quixote and
Sancho Panza encounter various adventures, whose accumulation and ordering constitute the structure of the narrative.
Indeed, it should not be surprising that Cervantes's novel was the
subject of an important instance of Russian Formalist literary
criticism, an essay by Shklovsky included in his volume *Theory of
Prose.* In his own cinematic reading of Cervantes's text,
Kozintsev also engages in an act of criticism, but of an
intertextual kind. Like Shklovsky, Kozintsev manages to illuminate the structure of the literary work of art in question.

Kozintsev clearly did not set out to undertake the "translation" of novel into film. In Formalist terms, it might be said that the novel is the film's material. But, as we have already suggested, the novel is seized upon for thematic reasons as well. Thus, for the Liehms, Kozintsev's *Don Quixote* stands as "the portrait of an honorable man fighting in vain against the cynicism that surrounds him."[6]

The Carnivalistic

Mikhail Bakhtin has usefully identified "Eccentricity" with the carnival attitude, as delineated in his great literary studies.[7] We have seen that the *avant-garde* films of the FEKS period were deeply carnivalistic in approach. Now, in this film of the final phase, the Cervantes adaptation, Kozintsev again evinces a predilection for carnivalism and its techniques. It might be said that Kozintsev structures his filmic text on the basis of a deeply felt sense of the carnival attitude and all that it implies. The carnivalistic attitude, it must be recalled, is never simple negation. In the parodic world of the carnivalistic, all certainty and exactness are banished. Carnival logic is that of "the world upside down."[7] The province of fixed meaning is rendered obsolete. The world becomes readable in multiple ways. In the carnival itself, this potential for the multiplicity of meanings is not difficult to explain: if, during the period of the carnival, a peasant may suddenly be crowned as a king, it does not mean that he is not also, at the same time, a peasant. And, indeed, the king who is uncrowned and functions now as a peasant still retains the shadow or trace of his kingly existence. Thus the play world of the carnival asserts duality, not merely the dominance of one reality over another. The carnival mask is another fascinating example of this phenomenon. The man wearing a mask has two faces, not one. The effect of the copresence implicit in the ambivalence of the carnival is that the alternation produces an effect of what Bakhtin calls "mutual bestrangement." The two components of the pair operate, then, to contest each other. Central tactics of the carnival are inversion and reversal, debasement and familiarization, "mésalliances, disguises and mystifications, contrasting paired images, scandals, drowning and discrownings."[8] Kozintsev's prior acquaintance with such techniques during the earlier FEKS days was now to prepare him for an encounter with Cervantes's text. For Bakhtin, *Don Quixote* is a literary work shot through with the carnivalistic attitude. Bakhtin argues that Cervantes's novel "is directly organized as a grotesque play with all its attributes. The depth and consequent nature of his realism are also typical of this pathos of change and renewal."[9] It is therefore quite fitting that in his cinematic adaptation of the text, Kozintsev laid bare this element of carnivalism.

The film begins with a tracking shot up and over the tops of the buildings of a Spanish town. The initial image is not problematized at once. This first scene is straightforward and simple—the passive contemplation of a world deemed to be "natural." By the time we reach the final image of the film, however—another landscape, but this time, ironically, an open craggy desert scene—our relationship to the world of the film will have undergone a radical metamorphosis. It is this complex process, whereby our relationship with the film's world is problematized, that is one of the film's most impressive aesthetic achievements. The stability, the closed form, of Socialist Realism—so long absolutely dominant in the Soviet cinema—is here contested and subverted by the ambivalence animated by the carnivalistic attitude. That stasis and finality which was, in essence, the aspiration of Socialist Realist art are the antithesis of the pervasive ambivalence of the filmic world of *Don Quixote*. As the film draws to an end, Don Quixote returns home from his quest. We see him there as he dreams of his better world in which he will defend justice forever. As he lies down on his pillow, we see the screen fill with the twilight landscape into which Don Quixote and Sancho Panza ride. The film, then, concludes as the pair proceeds into the distance. Now the final shot of the distant figures of Don Quixote and his companion might, out of context, seem to be a typical banal ending of any number of *kitsch* Socialist Realist productions. Here, though, the final shot may or may not be Quixote's dream—indeed, it no longer matters. By the time we reach this final sequence, dream and reality interpenetrate. The line between the two is blurred, rendered ambiguous, as it is in the ambience of the carnival. Alternate readings of the image are available to us. The manner in which Kozintsev manages to achieve this interpretation is of enormous interest, especially because we have so often been absolutely assured of a close bond between filmic image and reality. In a sense, then, Kozintsev's *Don Quixote* operates to provide a rigorous critique of filmic reality. It is a critique that would surely be forbidden in the Socialist Realist cinema with its aspiration toward the transparent text.

The narrative of Kozintsev's *Don Quixote* is animated initially through an absence. Before we actually view them, we listen to people talking about Don Quixote and his books, those "cursed books" in which he buries himself in tales of chivalry. Thus, through dialogue, Don Quixote assumes a certain intersubjective status. Yet, before we even meet him for the first time, Don Quixote is carnivalized, rendered ambivalent, provided with a mask. We hear that he has only recently assumed the name of Don Quixote, thereby abandoning his real name which would root him in the quotidian world. We hear, moreover, that, though his body lives in this quotidian world, his mind is in the fiction of his books. The figure of Don Quixote will, then, embody a fundamental duality, a carnivalistic ambivalence. When we finally get our first glimpse of Don Quixote, it is from the back, as he climbs out of the window of his room—a room crammed with books, and hence with fictions—and enters another world, one which will lose its stability or fixed meaning with his entrance.

Outside, wrapped in a black cloak and topped by a wide-brimmed hat that nearly masks his face, Don Quixote hears a sound. At first, we are unsure as to what the source of this sound is, for it remains off-screen. Soon, though, a pigherd enters the frame, and we realize that he is the source of the sound that has puzzled us. Don Quixote, however, has just suggested that the sound is a fanfare, perhaps heralding his arrival. Now, the appearance of the pigherd suggests a somewhat ironic disparity between expectation and reality. Indeed, the fanfare which Don Quixote names is the tune played by the pigherd's flute. Interestingly, now, Don Quixote does not alter his incorrect interpretation. His private world collides with what we see to be the case. The disparity demonstrates that which the townspeople were discussing earlier in the film concerning Don Quixote's refusal to leave his world of books for reality. Here, the visual image suggests the quotidian world, while Don Quixote's words suggest an imaginary one.

Word and Image

When a young peasant girl appears right after the pigherd incident, another collision between word and image occurs, in the form of a marked disparity between the girl herself and that which Don Quixote says about her. Here, though, an even more interesting ambivalence is suggested. Don Quixote speaks of the peasant girl as his beloved noblewoman Dulcinea. Now, however, we are no longer so sure that his criteria for truth are the product of simple madness. Don Quixote says that the young lady's qualities are those of a princess—goodness and kindness. Thus, for Don Quixote, it is not the mere accident of birth which makes Dulcinea a beloved noblewoman, but her genuine nobility of character. And, in fact, we do see this rather noble spirit in her. Her image, then, has been rendered ambivalent. She is, we see, *both* a peasant and Dulcinea! Here, then, is that technique of the carnival, as delineated by Bakhtin.

Carnival tactics are utilized in the initial view of Sancho Panza. First, there is a shot not of his face—as we might expect—but of his enormous buttocks. The visual pun is comic indeed in its suggestion that the poor fellow is an "ass." And, in a masterful touch, the comedy is intensified when the shot of Sancho Panza's enormous rear end is punctuated by a shot of the tiny naked buttocks of a child who scampers through the frame. Here, then, is an ironic doubling. The exaggeration of such bodily imagery is a favorite tactic of the carnivalistic work of art. Bakhtin has discussed it definitively in the work of Rabelais, but he also alludes to its presence in such authors as Shakespeare and, significantly, Cervantes. For Bakhtin, "the essential principle of grotesque realism is degradation, that is, the lowering of all that is high, spiritual, ideal, abstract; it is a transfer to the material level, to the sphere of earth and body in their indissoluble unity."[10]

With the important addition of Sancho Panza, a new stage is reached in the exploration of the disparity possible between word and image, dream and reality. Inevitably, Don Quixote and Sancho Panza will see and describe quite different things. And the effect of their contradictory readings of the same material will be that "alternation and mutual bestrangement" which Bakhtin identifies with the carnivalistic attitude. While Sancho Panza's reading of the material on the screen at a given moment will indeed be closer to what we actually see, the alternative description provided by Don Quixote will place us at a distance from this material, thereby defamiliarizing it somewhat. Moreover, the disparity operates to make the act of perception itself perceptible. The naturalness of the cinematic image is brilliantly subverted!

Before Don Quixote and Sancho Panza set off on their parodic quest, the dreamer must entrance his more mundane friend. Thus we watch as Don Quixote regales Sancho Panza with tales of the glory they will no doubt find. There is a distinct disjunction between the seductive poetic verbiage which we hear and that which we see—two rather clownish fellows in tattered clothing. Again—and ironically—word and image collide. Moreover, Don Quixote tells Sancho Panza what will be said of them in the future. That is, he talks about the book which will be written about them. In this manner, he offers—in advance— an alternate reading of the material which we will see in the course of the film. When Don Quixote thus inscribes his adventures into some *other* future narrative, we encounter a situation similar to that which Roland Barthes has discerned in Fourier, the case of the "metabook": "The meta-book is the book that talks about the book. Fourier spends his time talking about this book in such a way that the work of Fourier that we read, indissolubly blending the two discourses, finally forms an autonomous book, in which form incessantly states form."[11] This phenomenon, as described by Barthes, is to be discovered in Kozintsev's film in those moments when Don Quixote alludes to a future book and its interpretation of the events in the narrative that unrolls before us. Thus, the discourse of the film is here problematized on yet another level.

When Don Quixote and Sancho Panza set out finally, their quest is initiated by a comic subversion. As they ride off, Don Quixote's hat blows off. In this ironic touch, the glory of their departure is undercut. The knight and his quest are rendered familiar, as he will be again in a few moments, when he topples from his horse. This familiarization is another typical strategy of the carnival. The carnivalistic hero is not, however, thoroughly undermined by the many devices used to bring him down to earth. For Bakhtin has pointed out that though there is nothing stiff or stilted about this hero, this still "in no way harms the genuinely heroic core of the image."[12] Bakhtin's insight is clearly

applicable to Kozintsev's treatment of Don Quixote in the film.
No more are we given the wooden perfection of the almost
godlike positive heroes of the Socialist Realist cinema;
Kozintsev's depiction of character is something entirely different. The hero is indeed still heroic—but in a far more authentic
sense.

When Don Quixote topples from his horse, there is another
instance of the disparity between word and image. Don Quixote
perceives his fall as the work of Freston—the monster he
believes to have put a spell on the world and who is the enemy
he must defeat. Sancho, however, attributes the fall to a
quagmire known to all the townspeople.

A shot of a carriage on a journey animates yet another such
disparity. Don Quixote says that it is the "devil's chariot," but we
see only a carriage, precisely what Sancho Panza says that it is.
Yet, as was the case earlier in his encounter with the peasant girl,
there is a sense in which it is Don Quixote's reading which is
correct. For the noblewoman and her companions in the carriage
will indeed turn out to be devils of a sort. At times, then, Don
Quixote's fantastic outlook suggests valid metaphoric
possibilities. Now, Don Quixote charges down to the carriage
with the idea of saving a lady in distress. That play-acting which
has long been a thematic obsession of Kozintsev's is evident here.
For, indeed, the lady "plays" the kidnapped damsel for Don
Quixote. Then, when she undertakes a mock seduction of the
knight of the sorrowful countenance, it is a cruel parody of the
courtly love he affirms. This play-acting is another typical
feature of the carnival world. In the period of carnivalistic
license, there is the possibility of shifting roles freely. In
Kozintsev's *Don Quixote*, this stress on play-acting is also linked
to an aspect of its narrative structure—its episodic character.
Like the novel on which it is based, the film is episodic in
structure; many of its episodes look like theatrical tableaux.
They are indeed highly artificial and theatrical, played against
the backdrop of the sky. In this regard, for instance, we may
consider the scenes in which Don Quixote and Sancho Panza
discover a man beating his shepherd boy against a tree. The
confrontation is set up like a tableau in an artificial,
theatricalized setting. The way in which it is played out is almost
balletic in character. It is the space of play-acting, the scene in

which reversals may take place. Theater becomes a metaphor for the interpenetration of dream and reality.

The reversals enacted in this ludic locale may be disconcerting indeed. Thus, when Don Quixote saves a group of prisoners, their response to his kindness shatters all expectations in its carnivalistic reversal. Rather than expressing their gratitude to the man who has liberated them, all values are turned topsy-turvy, and they proceed to beat and berate their liberator.

The Thematics of Illusion

With Don Quixote and Sancho Panza's arrival at the country inn, a second phase in the film's treatment of illusion is reached. This episode seems to be initiated in the same fashion as in previous scenes, in which there is a clearcut disparity between word and image, between what Don Quixote says and what we, in fact, see. Don Quixote announces that they have arrived at a castle. We, however, see the locale to be that of an inn. The inn suggests a play world, the realm of the carnivalistic. All sorts of colorful riffraff are gathered there in order to drink, dance, and—of course—play various games. There is much card-playing and hints of sexual activity. The arrival of Don Quixote and Sancho Panza and his announcement of who he is meet with a mocking response, the laughter of the tarts, which serves to subvert his statement. The carnival, as we know, encourages plenty of subversive laughter. The present sequence recalls the atmosphere of FEKS, for it is peopled with grotesque figures. And for FEKS, the grotesque was a special preoccupation. In the dance sequence at the inn in Kozintsev's *Don Quixote,* the castinets click, and a man with a wooden leg dances with one of the tarts. Across the screen passes a figure walking on his hands! At one point at the inn, there is a close-up of a man slipping a playing card into his hat, thereby cheating at a game of cards. And again there is the comic disparity posited when a fat washerwoman climbs into bed thinking that Don Quixote is Sancho Panza. The scene is highly comic when Don Quixote calls her a countess, in yet another instance of ironic disparity.

But the film's treatment of the theme of illusion takes a new turn in the sequence which depicts Don Quixote in the cellar of the inn. He is shown speaking to the riffraff, telling them that all

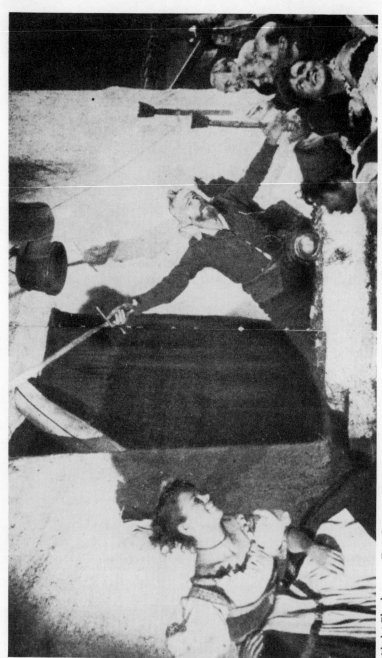

Nikolai Cherkasov as Don Quixote

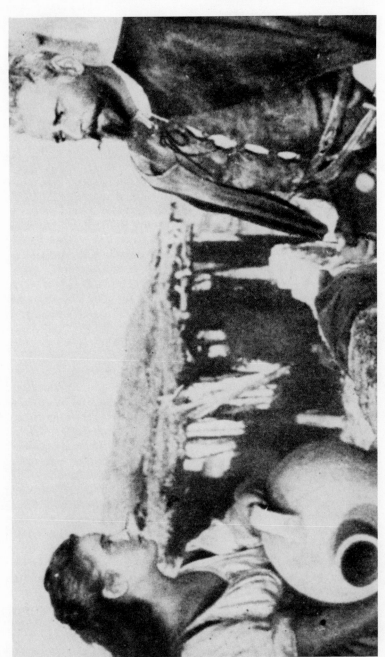

Quixote with Dulcinea

who do not see what he sees are under the spell of the monster
Freston. Then, a trap door—recalling, perhaps, elements of
Constructivist stage design popular during the *avant-garde*
period—suddenly opens, and Don Quixote tumbles onto a pile of
hay in the cellar beneath. The cellar becomes the space of
illusion. Now, for the first time in the film, we see what Don
Quixote sees, as well as the reality upon which his vision is based.
The camera moves over sacks of wine lined up in the cellar. As
we watch, the sacks metamorphose before our eyes. Like Don
Quixote, we see the sacks become grotesque faces. The faces
now stick out their tongues in a gesture of carnivalistic ridicule.
Thus the sacks of wine come alive, performing a kind of mock
ballet. Don Quixote stabs them repeatedly, causing wine to pour
all over the cellar. For Don Quixote, this is not wine, but blood.
This frenzied stabbing provides a show at which the people of
the inn laugh uproariously. Here, again, is the theme of play-
acting; Don Quixote's encounter with the sacks of wine is
theatricalized; it is rendered into an entertainment. The mocking
riffraff operate here as our own doubles. We, too, have laughed
uproariously at Don Quixote throughout the film thus far. Now,
however, we have seen that which he sees. The reality posited
by the film begins to dissolve.

After his travels, when the battered knight returns home for
the first time, it is jarring indeed when a visitor to the town
inquires about Don Quixote. After all, "Don Quixote"is only an
assumed name. Illusion has thus begun to contest quotidian
reality. Perhaps the sequence in which we have shared Don
Quixote's vision has prepared us for the strange moment of doubt
we experience now. In asking for Don Quixote, the horseman
bestows a certain reality upon this *persona*, this fiction. The
illusion acquires a degree of intersubjectivity. Don Quixote's
hitherto private view of the world is shared by another. But in a
moment we discover that it is all the doing of the lady from the
carriage encountered in an earlier sequence. Now, she has come
to take Don Quixote with her to the court of the duke. It is all a
cruel joke. Again, she pretends to be overwhelmed with love for
the aging knight. In fact, though, she merely plans to use him for
the purpose of the amusement of the court. In the course of the
journey, the entourage encounters a wagon carrying a lion. Don
Quixote proceeds to engage in a touching discourse with the
mighty beast, speaking of how lonely and out of place each of

them is in Spain. This encounter between Don Quixote and the lion suggests Kozintsev's attitude toward the Fool as a type, an attitude which would later play a significant role in the director's last film, *King Lear*. Indeed, Kozintsev felt enormous sympathy for the Fool as a character type. Throughout *Don Quixote,* this sympathy may in fact be discerned. But the encounter with the lion is perhaps its most touching and forceful instance.

The scenes at the ducal court mark a third phase in Kozintsev's exploration of the tension between illusion and reality. In the first phase, we recall, there is a clearcut disparity between illusion and reality, word and image. In the second phase, we actually see that which Don Quixote sees. In this third phase, then, no trickery is needed to underscore the disparity between Don Quixote's illusion and what is really there. We see what the knight sees, but we are aware—as he is not—that what we see is illusion, mere play-acting. The members of the court stage the illusion in question here. Thus, by this three-phase treatment of the thematics of illusion, Kozintsev solves an aesthetic problem; that is, he manages to sustain interest in his exploration by varying its course somewhat.

Previously, Don Quixote had imagined himself in a world of splendor; now, his environment is in fact quite opulent. The illusion is far more subtle in this segment. Here, illusion is a function of play-acting. The court only pretends to view Don Quixote as a serious knight. In fact, he is viewed as something of a jester. The irony of this disparity is intensified because this time we cannot actually see the disjunction between Don Quixote's illusion and what is actually there.

At the court, the presence of the dwarf jester is a carnivalistic detail. And, typically, it is the jester who is the voice of truth. The dwarf predicts that Don Quixote will not stay long among the fools of the court, for Don Quixote is no fool! Thus, the dwarf jester posits another reading of the material—a reading which appears to reverse the apparent signification of the sequence. It is his word which animates the carnivalistic reversal.

Now the duke awards Sancho Panza a prize that suggests the inversions associated with carnivalism by fulfilling his wish to become the governor of his own island. This, by the way, is the prize which the sorrowful knight had used to convince Sancho Panza to set out on the quest in the first place. As Sancho Panza and Don Quixote exit from the court, they leave together with the nobles; the rule of carnival that all distance between participants be abolished is here observed. On the island, the reversal characteristic of carnival license takes place; the lowly becomes the ruler. Mounted on his donkey, Sancho Panza rides in dressed in mock splendor, much to the amusement of the spectators. The locus of the island, however, suggests a frame, which marks off a kind of playground where the rules are different, an area for ludic activity. The motif of play is picked up in the image of children in the square playing at bullfighting. One kind of play echoes another. When the period of play rule is over, Sancho leaves with a rude gesture to the nobles; he slaps his rear and sticks out his tongue. Indeed, no one in the world of carnival is immune to ridicule. Laughter is ambivalent, as well. Bakhtin has remarked that "the people's festive laughter . . . is also directed at those who laugh." This is precisely the case here.

Don Loco

Meanwhile, at the court, Don Quixote has been the butt of another cruel joke. He is told that the noblewoman who brought him to the duke has died of unrequited love for him. The courtiers then proceed to stage an elaborate mock funeral scene. The sequence is played with such enormous restraint that it is positively unsettling. In particular, the behavior of the duke and the duchess is especially strange. Neither one laughs uproariously at the farce they have staged. Indeed, they betray only the slightest trace of a smirk. When the joke is at last revealed, the duke tells Don Quixote that it was merely a jest, "a farce like everything else in this world." The world is a stage; life, a dream. As the nobles applaud, the effect of their highly ordered response is eerie, dream-like. The scene assumes an oneiric character. Crushed, Don Quixote leaves. But before he does so, he pauses for a moment before an enormous tapestry on which is depicted a knight in armor, mounted on a horse, and carrying a lance. As the two knights share the frame, the disparity between the image and what Don Quixote really is comes into focus. The dwarf has placed a card on Don Quixote's back; it labels him "Don Loco."

After leaving the court, Don Quixote is reunited with Sancho Panza. Now, the knight engages in what will be his final battle — the imaginary conquest of the evil monster Freston, whom he believes has cast a spell on the world. Kozintsev returns us to the initial treatment of the tension between illusion and reality. We clearly see Don Quixote charging a windmill—the windmill, by the way, which is prefigured in the drawing under the opening titles of the film. Don Quixote, however, sees not a windmill, but Freston the monster. The windmill operates metaphorically, of course, for it suggests the workaday world against which Don Quixote's vision must struggle.

Persuaded to return home by his doctor—only after the latter, in disguise, has defeated him in a knightly joust—Don Quixote now encounters a disturbing series of repetitions of earlier sequences. He meets another gang of chained prisoners, for instance. Then, he encounters the little shepherd boy whom he thought he had saved from a beating. Now, however, the lad berates Don Quixote for the even more dreadful beating he subsequently received after the knight's interference. This quite ironic recapitulation of Don Quixote's early encounters animates a cruel subversion of his vision. Parodic doubling deflates the past in carnivalistic fashion. Don Quixote, however, somehow manages to remain a positive force. At home, he dreams that Dulcinea and Sancho Panza beg him not to give up his cause. Thus he affirms that justice will triumph and that he will never retreat. Then, he sinks back onto his pillows. Kozintsev cuts to an empty landscape, across which the camera moves. It is into the distance of this landscape that Don Quixote and Sancho Panza appear to ride. As the film concludes, there is again the picture of the windmill. But the repetition is not without its difference. This time the windmill is depicted without the threatening blades which turned at the start. It would seem that Don Quixote has vanquished the monster.

Homo Ludens

After the era of Socialist Realism, a novel about reality and realism like Cervantes's *Don Quixote* was a shrewd choice for cinematic adaptation. Kozintsev's *Don Quixote*, seizes upon the milieu of play and games as a central concern. This essential thematic in the filmic text raises issues of representation and realism. Thus Kozintsev's *Don Quixote* may be read as a reflexive text. As such, it operates to scrutinize itself and its context, aesthetic and social. This is not to allegorize the text; yet elements in the diegesis do in fact raise issues relevant to the time and place in which the film was made. What, then, is the relevance of Kozintsev's concern with *homo ludens*?

The present century has witnessed a great deal of philosophical speculation about the role of play and games in life. For some writers—at once, Johan Huizinga comes to mind—art-making is identified with play. It is not merely, however, the "fantastic" artist who plays with his materials. Indeed, we may say that the so-called "realist" artist plays as much as any other. In an incisive remark, Jacques Ehrmann has noted that "all reality is caught up in the play of the concepts which designate it." Talking about writing, Ehrmann goes on to say that it is not the literary critic's job to sort out the "realistic" from the "unrealistic."[13] In thematizing issues of play and reality, Kozintsev's *Don Quixote* in fact, frustrates such an approach.

In treating play, the film posits a series of play worlds—to borrow a term from Eugen Fink.[14] The "play world" is a mirror structure, a *mise en abyme*. It subverts and calls into question any purported "realism" of the text that circumscribes it. In this attention to homo ludens, Kozintsev animates his most decisive carnivalistic strategy. With his vision, his intrinsic contestation of reality, Don Quixote is the type of the man who plays. He even suggests, perhaps, the artist as player. A repressive world of conventions circumcribes his play world. Significantly, Fink has pointed out "two extreme modes of being" that are available to the player. These two modes are quite relevant to the problems examined in Kozintsev's text. One mode posited by Fink is "a pinnacle of human sovereignty." This mode—obviously quite desirable indeed—is characterized by great creativity. Such creativity suggests, perhaps, the artist as player. But Fink also delineates another extreme mode. This is "the opposite pole of freedom, a withdrawal from the real world, which can go so far as enchantment and trance and reach a point of total enslavement through the demonic power of the mask."[15] This other, rather forbidding pole is taken up in Cervantes's book. So, too, it is an important concern of the film under consideration. In both cases—Cervantes and Kozintsev—the work of art treats, but certainly does not exemplify this other pole, "total enslavement through the demonic power of the mask." Against the cinema of Socialist Realism, then, Kozintsev poses the play world of art, creativity, "a pinnacle of human sovereignty."

Cherkasov has recalled that Kozintsev explained his image of the knight by saying that he "is not just a madman—he is kind and just." Kozintsev's Don Quixote is, then, treated with a certain carnivalistic ambivalence. The diegesis depicts both poles, freedom and its opposite. This structural aspect of Kozintsev's *Don Quixote* is, perhaps, its most remarkable achievement.

With *Don Quixote*, the director initiates the final phase of his career. In his next two films—the concluding works of his *oeuvre*—Kozintsev would turn from Cervantes to another giant of world literature, William Shakespeare. In *Hamlet*, the film that followed *Don Quixote*, the shifting roles of men at "play" would again be the director's concern.

5

Hamlet

SHAKESPEARE'S HAMLET had intrigued Kozintsev for many years when, in 1964, he adapted it to the cinema. Apparently, in the *avant-garde* period of the 1920s, Kozintsev suggested to Sergei Gerassimov the possibility of adapting the play in the FEKS style. Kozintsev advised a "modern tempo" for the work, which would be rendered in pantomime (*STC*, p. 211).[1] Such a strategy would surely operate to defamiliarize the classic text. Years later, in 1953–54, Kozintsev staged a theatrical production of *Hamlet* at the Pushkin Academic Theater in Leningrad. In addition, Kozintsev was the author of a particularly rich body of criticism on Shakespeare, which included incisive commentaries on *Hamlet*, with indications of the director's aesthetic approach to the problem of its production. Then, in 1964, *Hamlet* became a film, which may itself be read in relation to Kozintsev's previous preoccupation with Shakespeare's text. This film, with a celebrated score by Dmitri Shostakovich, is certainly one of Kozintsev's best, and a major contribution to the canon of Shakespearean film.

Alluding to his intensive involvement with Shakespeare's play, Kozintsev has remarked in his journal that "there are certain books which you cannot claim to 'have read'; you 'are reading' Shakespeare every time" (*STC*, p. 225). Thus Kozintsev suggests that the enterprise of reading certain texts is nothing less than an ongoing process, an encounter between the self and literary structure. He goes on to note that, with both a theatrical production and a critical study of *Hamlet* already to his credit, he was "still reading *Hamlet*" at the time of the film project (*STC*, p. 225). Indeed, new meanings were still to be produced in the course of this sustained encounter with Shakespeare. As reader,

95

Kozintsev was still to discover new things in the text before him. We may say that each of Kozintsev's creative approaches to the text—theatrical production, literary criticism, and now cinematic adaptation—was, in a sense, an interpretative operation, a strategy for comprehending *Hamlet*. Roland Barthes, in his critical study *S/Z*, has proposed the need to become a producer rather than a consumer of the text. Here, Barthes suggests a critical methodology, a way of reading. Is this not Kozintsev's tactic in relation to *Hamlet?* In order to read the text, Kozintsev "produces" it—theatrically, critically, cinematically. Moreover, in *S/Z*, Barthes has indicated the need for rereading, an activity which, as he points out, is discouraged in a society dominated by consumption. Once completed, the text must be discarded in order that the consumer may move on to another. This is precisely the situation to which Kozintsev alludes when he suggests the impossibility of truly being finished with certain texts. Such texts are not to be consumed, but read, reread, and produced. Each of Kozintsev's *Hamlet* texts, then, posits rereadings in the best sense. Barthes identifies rereading not with consumption, but with play. Thus it might be said that Kozintsev plays with *Hamlet* in each of his rereadings.

In his journal Kozintsev suggests that the text contained a certain personal significance for him: *"Hamlet* is for me a work that includes everything that I have loved throughout my life, everything to which I have aspired since childhood, albeit still unconsciously—the forms of expressions and feelings and thoughts (those I understood much later): from the wandering players to the theme of man and time" (*STC*, p. 275). The critic who wished to undertake a psychoanalytic study of Kozintsev's films—along the lines, perhaps, of Dominique Fernandez's book on Eisenstein—might well seize upon this statement as an interesting point of departure. This, however, is not the tactic of the present study. It ought to be remarked that the text never functions as a mere mirror for Kozintsev. Instead, the director *actively* engages in the production of textual meaning. When Kozintsev argues that the play must not be produced, but suffered, he is suggesting precisely this active engagement with its system. The notion of suffering recalls the vocabulary of Antonin Artaud, a theoretician of some interest to Kozintsev. Kozintsev's deeply felt experience of *Hamlet* is registered in his successive rereadings. The film, then, is not an index of some reality, but, rather, of the director's encounter with Shakespeare's text.

At this juncture, it is necessary to consider for a moment how an artist's journals may be useful in criticism. The issue, of course, has been debated widely. In Anglo-American criticism, the intentional fallacy was definitively analyzed and rejected by Wimsatt and Beardsley in *The Verbal Icon.* Surely, then, an artist's journals are not to be used merely to discover his intentions! For the critic, they may, however, perform another, quite useful function. The relevant debate here would be that between the two Russian Formalist critics, Shklovsky and Eikhenbaum. Reading Shklovsky's collage text *Third Factory,* we come upon a vigorous attack on the use of diaries in critical practice. For Shkovsky, then, "diaries lead us into the psychology of the creative process and the question of the laboratory of the genius." The section of *Third Factory* in question here is a letter to another Formalist writer, Tynianov, which forms part of the text's overall collage. Shklovsky asks Tynianov to show the letter to "Boris," who is, of course, Boris Eikhenbaum. This should be clear from the line which announces that "one must write not about Tolstoy, but about *War and Peace."* Here Shklovsky refers to Eikhenbaum's critical methodology in his study of Tolstoy, in which he makes extensive use of the author's diaries. Thus Shklovsky attacks the notion that it is critically relevant to scrutinize the relations between the artist and his work. For Shklovsky, "one must study not the problematical connection but the facts."[2] It must be said, however, that although Eikhenbaum does indeed devote much attention to Tolstoy's diaries, he is extremely rigorous in his methodology and never lapses into what would later be called the intentional fallacy. What role, then, do the diaries play in Eikhenbaum's study? And how is this tactic possibly instructive for criticism in general? The question is important here because of the existence of Kozintsev's own personal records concerning his encounter with Shakespeare. What critical use may we tactfully make of them? Eikhenbaum, then, proposes that a study of Tolstoy's texts ought to begin with the diaries, which are characterized by "an intense and ceaseless self-observation and awareness." But, with typical methodological tact, Eikhenbaum proceeds to suggest the danger of an interpretation that is merely psychological. For Eikhenbaum, "it is not a matter of Tolstoy's nature, but of the acts of his creative

consciousness. . . ." Thus, instead of a psychological scrutiny of
the diaries, Eikhenbaum proposes to attend to a " 'formal' upper
stratum."[3] In the present study of the two great works produced
through Kozintsev's encounter with Shakespeare, it is precisely
this " 'formal' upper stratum" which is seized upon in the diaries.
In turn, the diaries are situated intertextually in relation to the
films themselves. The diaries and the films participate in
Kozintsev's construction of "Shakespeare," a new reading of
texts gathered under this name.

Shakespeare as Script-Writer

Kozintsev's *Hamlet* is widely recognized for its cinematic
excellence, as well as for its extremely intelligent approach to
the problems of adaptation. Here Kozintsev used a translation by
Boris Pasternak, which was itself a creative interpretation of
Shakespeare's text; indeed, the significance of Pasternak's
translations for Kosintsev's Shakespeare films, *Hamlet* and *King
Lear*, must not be underestimated. Kozintsev once commented,
"for some time Shakespeare has been much in demand as a
script-writer" (*STC*, p. 28). This witty remark suggests
Kozintsev's interest in the issues of Shakespearean adaptation in
general. As we shall see, his writings clearly evince a knowledge
of other approaches to this task, in relation to which Kozintsev's
own Shakespeare films may be considered. Thus Kozintsev's
Hamlet, as well as his *King Lear*, engage us in issues of
intertextuality. Most evident is the intertextual encounter of
Kozintsev and Shakespeare. Kozintsev's adaptations posit a
strong reading. As his recorded theoretical speculations suggest,
Kozintsev was a gifted critic, acutely aware of the essential
limitations of any reading. With regard to *Hamlet*, Kozintsev
wrote that the most valuable things in the play remain somehow
beyond our conception. The critic Tzvetan Todorov has pointed
out the manner in which any reading never quite "reaches" the
text in question. Instead, it appears to be ever approaching the
text. A strong sense of this endless approach to *Hamlet* is felt in
the journal which Kozintsev kept during his work on the film
version. Although the journal refers most directly to the
cinematic project itself, it may also be regarded as literary
criticism at its best. The restless, fragmented character of the
journal entries suggests that "continual oscillation between the

analyzed text and theory" which Todorov ascribes to the enterprise of reading.[4] For Todorov, a reading aspires to detect the system of the text. Since Kozintsev's Shakespeare films are themselves readings, they may be said to provide new insights into the systems of the texts in question.

Indeed, Kozintsev himself wished to go beyond the mere construction of "film versions." In this term, Kozintsev discerned "something lifeless and mechanistic" (*STC*, p. 260). The notion, rejected by Kozintsev, suggests for him that "it's as though you put a literary work into a slot in some computerlike machine and push the button: a snap of the fingers, the noise of levers and wheels, and from another aperture the reels of film come rolling out" (*STC*, p. 260). According to Kozintsev, the sorry result of such an operation would be merely some "prefab product." Kozintsev's metaphor of the "computerlike machine" suggests, perhaps, the Russian Formalist notion of automatized experience. The Russian Formalist critics argued that the tactic of art is to deautomatize experience. In this regard, Kozintsev moves to deautomatize the Shakespearean text. The "prefab product"— the automatized text—is to be avoided. Stale, worn-out conventions and conceptions must be discarded. Cinematic adaptations of classic literary works are too often little more than examples of *kitsch*. In such cases, the film itself has little aesthetic interest; instead, it is merely a means to an end, presenting the aura of the classic text. The filmic text remains transparent, or at least aspires to do so. Derivative adaptations of this sort are lifeless indeed and possess little interest within the context of cinema. Kozintsev's adaptations, on the contrary, are, above all else, films in the best sense, which make full use of the possibilities of the medium.

In the course of working on the film version of *Hamlet*, Kozintsev felt that he had never experienced such a great need to "revise the methods of expression" utilized in previous films (*STC*, p. 269). Thus, even the "methods of expression" were to be deautomatized, reconsidered. In Russian Formalist criticism, deautomatization refers not just to the represented world, but to devices themselves. Kozintsev's procedure, then, was marked by a continuous reflexivity. The director speculated as to whether his need to reconsider previous methods derived from the advent of new cinematic devices and decided that this was not the case. Instead, Kozintsev determined that it was because he

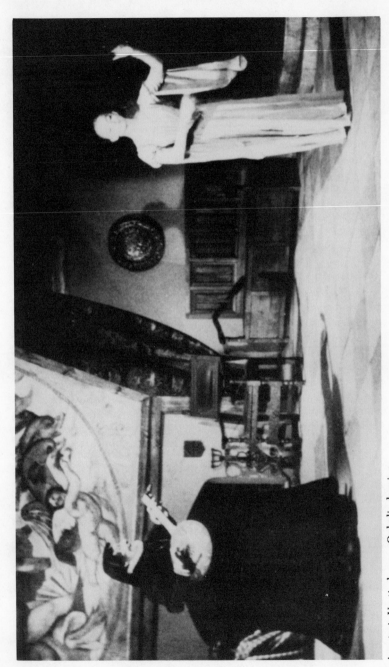

Anastasia Vertinskaya as Ophelia dancing

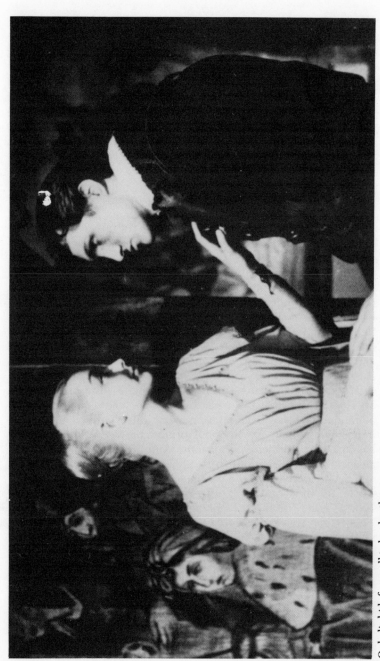

Ophelia bids farewell to her brother

had discovered "in a sixteenth-century play a modern and novel story about life, history and man" (*STC*, p. 269). If Kozintsev thought of his film version of *Hamlet* in relation to other films in his own *oeuvre*, he also considered it in terms of the work of other filmmakers. Thus, another sort of intertextuality operative here involves the relation between Kozintsev and other directors in world cinema who have sought to use Shakespeare as their script-writer. In his writing, Kozintsev will frequently allude to efforts in this regard by such diverse artists as Kurosawa, Brook, Olivier, or Zeffirelli.

James Billington has located Kozintsev's *Don Quixote* and *Hamlet* in relation to prior Russian readings: "In contrast to Turgenev's 'Hamlet and Don Quixote' of almost a century before, Kozintsev depicted Quixote as a psychologically disturbed and tragic figure, and gave to Hamlet a certain quiet nobility. Like Pasternak (whose translation of the play was used for the script), Kozintsev seemed to be vindicating Hamlet from the symbolic opprobrium heaped on him by Turgenev (and the lesser critics of the Stalin era)."[5] Indeed, the play and its central figure, Hamlet, have long exercised a particular fascination for the Russians. In the nineteenth century, in particular, Hamlet and "Hamletism" became touchstones for discussions of the Russian character. Everyone—from the Radical Critic Belinsky to Herzen to Turgenev—seemed to recognize the proliferation of Hamlet-figures in Russia. Of course, each of the varied commentators saw Hamlet somewhat differently, but what is important is that the fictional prince became a metaphor in literary and political discussions. And Kozintsev was acutely aware of this Russian intertext; in his diary he wrote: "However much we might try to reproduce the English or the Danish world, the film—if it turns out—will be Russian. We still have our Hamlet from the times of Belinsky and Herzen" (*STC*, p. 243). This intertext is essential to any comprehension of Kozintsev's approach to the text. In his encounter with Shakespeare's play, moreover, Kozintsev was quite conscious of possible associations evoking Russian literature; thus, the "mousetrap" scene in *Hamlet* was described as "Lermontovian," while its end was "Pushkinian." For the Russian reader, Kozintsev, Shakespeare's world intersected with the worlds of great Russian writers. Obviously, such associations could not have occurred to a man named Shakespeare. But the historical man is less important in this regard than the place of his texts in a network of other texts. Thus, for Kozintsev, certain moments in *Hamlet*—the "mousetrap scene" or the end—are intertextual neighbors of the Russians, Lermontov and Pushkin. This is to view literature—as T. S. Eliot did, for instance—as an order, a system.

Another figure from the Russian literary canon in relation to whom Kozintsev situates Shakespeare is Dostoevsky. Indeed, Kozintsev has recalled the fact that an American review of the film version of *Hamlet* alluded to it as *"The Brothers Karamozov from Elsinore."* And, not surprisingly, Kozintsev has written insightful and provocative lines on Dostoevsky's idea of space—lines which suggest, perhaps, the director's own preoccupation with cinematic space. In commenting on the intertextual encounter of Shakespeare and Dostoevsky, Kozintsev observed: "I was fully aware that Dostoevsky's Petersburg had nothing in common with Shakespeare's Britain." What, then, we may ask, is the connection to be established between the two authors and their seemingly divergent texts? In answering this question, Kozintsev sets forth a principle of critical methodology which recalls insights encountered in the theoretical writings of Eliot and Borges. According to Kozintsev, "great discoveries in art influence not only the future but the past." Here we may think of the way in which Eliot suggested that great works of art actually modify our sense of previous works. An important new work alters that order established by prior monuments of art. For Borges, for example, the poetry of Browning may be comprehended in a new way *after* a reading of Kafka. Similarly, then, Kozintsev suggests that "one discovers new things in old books from reading a contemporary book." Works of art are not isolated; their meanings are produced in relation to each other. Thus Kozintsev suggests that "the 'fantastic realism' which Dostoevsky talked of so much (and which began with Gogol) was not only responsible for and forestalled much contemporary art, but opened up new aspects of the classics (and perhaps Shakespeare first and foremost) which no one had paid any attention to before" (*KL*, p. 90). We may recall the Poundian notion of "making it new," for this is precisely what happens when Dostoevsky and Shakespeare are crossed.

As J. P. Sullivan has written, "it is partly due to Pound with his insistence on 'making it new,' that we have freed ourselves from the inert Arnoldian conception of a classic, the belief that there

The gravedigging scene in *Hamlet*

is *one* Homer whose qualities are objectively there. . . ."[6]
Pound's strategy in this regard is Kozintsev's, as well. Before
opening a critical essay entitled "Hamlet and Hamletism,"
Kozintsev offers the reader a quotation from Romain Rolland's
Goethe and Beethoven which suggests the particular subtleties of
the reader's enterprise, including, of course, the artist as
intertextual reader: "Even when we return to works of the past
(different periods never select the same work from the great
storehouse of the past; yesterday it was Beethoven and Wagner,
today Bach and Mozart), it is not the past which revives in us; it is
we ourselves who cast our shadows into the past—our desires,
our order, and our confusion." Thus, as we shall see, Kozintsev's
Hamlet is not just a Russian one, but a very *contemporary* one, as
well. Kozintsev utilizes the citation from Rolland in order to
propose the particular complexity of his own reading of *Hamlet.*
Elsewhere, Kozintsev has written: "In Shakespeare plays—as in
everything created by man—certain aspects are closer to artists
of one nation or epoch, others to different ones. The rhetoric and
complex metaphors are what I feel to be most alien to us . . ."
(*KL,* p. 67). This comment, made with specific reference to *King
Lear,* applies, of course, in the case of *Hamlet,* as well. Here
again Kozintsev calls attention to the interpretive enterprise
involved in the cinematic adaptation of Shakespeare. On a
simpler level, the director was well aware of the fact that "any
foreigner who opens a film with the reproduction of everyday
details is destined to failure," (*KL,* p. 10). Thus he cites an
American version of *Anna Karenina* in whose opening moments
"caviar was spooned on to the plates with soup spoons." Surely
Kozintsev's adaptations of Shakespeare avoid such intrusions of
kitsch.

As a Russian reading Shakespeare, Kozintsev was generally
interested in the interplay that occurs when a filmmaker of one
nationality adapts to the screen a classic text of another. For
further insight into the complexities of this aesthetic problem,
Kozintsev—in the course of his writings—turned to the example
of the Japanese director Akira Kurosawa. One of Kurosawa's
adaptations, for instance, was of Dostoevsky's *The Idiot.*
Kozintsev carefully scrutinized this Japanese version of a Russian
novel for what it might reveal about such encounters. Kozintsev

remarked that Russians tend to view such foreign adaptations of their classics somewhat suspiciously. At times, of course, such suspicion might dissolve once the film was under way, and such was the case with Kozintsev's experience of Kurosawa's film. Although the film featured Japanese actors—such as the incomparable Toshiro Mifune, who played Rogozhin—and occurred in modern Japan, Kozintsev suddenly found himself in the world of Dostoevsky (*KL*, p. 10). Kozintsev found that "it was all outwardly different and yet completely the same in inner action, the same world that the author created." Thus Kozintsev discovers in Kurosawa that the important feature in adaptation— especially, perhaps, when the filmmaker is working with a foreign text—is "inner action." Outward details, it would appear, may be altered drastically. In fact, it seems that part of the power of Kurosawa's film is the manner in which it defamiliarizes Dostoevsky's material, while remaining faithful to that "inner action" valued by Kozintsev. These notions would be significant indeed to Kozintsev the director.

Like Kozintsev, Kurosawa has engaged in the adaptation of Shakespeare to the screen. It is, of course, in this capacity that his work holds special interest for his Russian counterpart. It is of enormous theoretical interest to observe this Russian observing the Japanese director observing, in turn, the greatest of English poets! Kozintsev found Kurosawa's version of *Macbeth*, entitled *Throne of Blood*, to be "the finest of Shakespearean movies" (*STC*, p. 29). Here, too, Japanese actors and the film's location in feudal Japan struck Kozintsev—as they probably do most viewers—as especially effective. For Kozintsev, in fact, the passion evinced by the actors—including, again, Toshiro Mifune—was quite different from anything to be discovered in European film or theatre. Kozintsev noted in the characters—in spite of an absence of "external verisimilitude in the perfor- mance of the actors"—an inner authenticity (*STC*, p. 30). Setting, as well, operated to "make it new," as Pound would say. Kozintsev reports—quite poetically, in fact—that, in *Throne of Blood*, "decor was sometimes no more than a patch of mould on a paper wall" (*KL*, p. 11). In Kurosawa's film, Kozintsev detected the influence of Japanese Noh Theatre. Here, then, was a revealing instance of intertextuality involving the collision of

cultural traditions. Kozintsev's own Shakespeare films—like
Kurosawa's *Throne of Blood*—mark an intertextual site, the
collision of cultures and traditions.

Important and Basic Things

Kozintsev greatly valued austerity and self-restraint as directorial qualities. Clearly, these were the traits to which he aspired
in his Shakespearean adaptations. The pristine look of *Hamlet*
and *King Lear* derives from this predilection for simplicity.
Wherever possible, extraneous ornament was to be removed.
Recognizing the difficulty of this form of self-denial, Kozintsev
nevertheless insisted upon its extreme importance for aesthetic
achievement. For Kozintsev, the director's task was, in essence,
"to guide the film to clusters of the important and basic things"
(*STC*, p. 236). Thus, the self-restraint which Kozintsev proposes
is, perhaps, a factor in achieving a more penetrating reading of
the text. Kozintsev writes of the need "to cleanse a director's
work of the bravura of gadgets, of the device annexed to
Shakespeare" (*STC*, p. 236). Manneristic strategies were clearly
to be avoided. Only that device which managed to reveal
something in the text was to be appropriated for the film. The
reference to "gadgets" suggests that, as fascinated by the
dazzling possibilities of the medium as he was, Kozintsev was
nevertheless wary of the gratuitous display of pyrotechnics.
Kozintsev noted that "the strength of the director does not lie in
an obstinate execution of every detail in his plan, but in
mercilessly throwing out everything personal, everything that
does not organically belong" (*STC*, p. 275). Thus Kozintsev
values the essential organicity of the text, literary or cinematic.
In a Borgesian sense, it is almost as if the text were to take on a
life of its own. It must be recalled that Kozintsev expressed a
personal involvement with Shakespeare's *Hamlet*. Thus it is
significant that in his journal he reminds himself of the absolute
necessity of discarding the personal when it does not fit. The
artist must not indulge himself. He must be rigorous in his
decisions, even at the expense of some of his initial plans.
Kozintsev argues that "life and ideas are the test and measure of
everything." Here, then, is the yardstick against which the
artist's labor may be measured. Accordingly, the artist finds
himself compelled "to strike out the superfluous, the lifeless, or

the empty of thought" (*STC*, p. 275). A wariness concerning the excessive and superficial is also evident in those journal entries written in conjunction with Kozintsev's theatrical production of *Hamlet* at the Pushkin Academic Theater in Leningrad. For the director, the "main enemies" were "pathos and bombast" (*STC*, p. 214). Moreover, he notes the necessity of avoiding "superficial romanticism" (*STC*, p. 218). Here, too, the aspiration is toward austerity and rigor.

Reflecting on his activity as a filmmaker, Kozintsev has recalled his long-term effort "to neutralize everything which has anything to do with ancient settings, to tone them down and make them less obtrusive" (*KL*, p. 1). For Kozintsev, the overly meticulous depiction of a period would involve a loss of an authentic sense of Shakespeare's imagery. Kozintsev felt himself to have actively opposed the aesthetic of the so-called "historical epic" since the Gogol adaptation of the FEKS period. Since *The Cloak*, Kozintsev had been preoccupied by a consideration of how cinematic means might be pressed into the service of an exploration of time past. In such an exploration, how might *kitsch* effects be avoided? The quest involved a rejection of the "historical" or the "costume" film. Moreover, Kozintsev argued against the "picturesque" as a cinematic strategy. The imitation of ancient paintings was also to be avoided. Kozintsev's solution to the aesthetic problem that confronted him in this regard was what he would term "the poetry of plastic sensation" (*STC*, p. 237). Kozintsev pointed to films such as *The Youth of Maxim* and *Don Quixote* in which, as he noted, "the reality of the particular epoch lays bare its own special expressiveness" (*STC*, p. 237). Thus the director strived to create a poetic means for seizing upon the essence of a milieu. The visual imagery developed in this exploration of the epoch would not be extraneous to the film as a whole. In the Cervantes adaptation, for instance, Kozintsev says that "the red wastes of la Mancha, burned by the sun, or the dead primness of the ducal court, are not devices but are included in the material itself" (*STC*, p. 237). In other words, the film's visual style is to be a reflection of its thematic concerns. Kozintsev is arguing critically against those films in which visual style is gratuitously developed.

Kozintsev considered the aesthetic problem of setting intertextually in relation to the practical decisions of other filmmakers engaged in the adaptation of Shakespearean texts. He reports never having "been convinced by the idea of filming Shakespeare in the actual settings of the plays, neither by Orson Welles's Venice nor Franco Zeffirelli's Verona" (*STC*, p. 80). In Kozintsev's view, "historical naturalism" was not the appropriate tactic in these cases. This critical approach, then, suggested his own technique as a filmmaker. Kozintsev posits that it would have been impossible for him to film his *Hamlet* in the castle of Elsinore itself. The notion is not as paradoxical as it may at first seem. Kozintsev notes that the real Castle of Elsinore "bears no resemblance at all to Claudius' kingdom." The poet, Kozintsev argues, evinced "the most approximate conception" of such locales in his texts as the Castle of Elsinore. This notion of Shakespeare determines, then, practical decisions with regard to Kozintsev's Shakespeare films. Kozintsev describes Elsinore as a "speculative concept" (*STC*, p. 265). The director's strategy in relation to the problem of rendering this "speculative concept" on screen was to avoid a view of the structure as a whole. Instead, the various parts of the edifice might be shown individually. The imagination of the audience would be put to work in developing a "general plan" of Elsinore (*STC*, p. 265). Various shots, registered in different locales, would be utilized, then, to create, through montage, a single imaginary space, that "speculative concept" of which Kozintsev speaks.

For Kozintsev, the world to be constructed in the film will be a whole, but nonexistent, one. In this, Kozintsev reflects Kuleshov's insights into the technique of montage. Kuleshov, we recall, suggested the possibility of creating nonexistent women out of bits and pieces of film, the various bodily parts rendered actually belonging to quite different individuals, but here providing the illusion of a single body. Thus Kuleshov demonstrated the remarkable creative power of montage. In his exploration of "creative geography," Kuleshov demonstrated the possibility of fabricating quite imaginary locales, nonexistent in the world as we know it. Such locales would be created out of bits and pieces of different places, actually existing in the everyday world at great distances from each other. In *Hamlet,* then, Kozintsev seized upon the findings of Kuleshov: "Hamlet took his first steps in our film on the shores of the Baltic Sea and his second step by the Black Sea; there were several hours of flying time between the two" (*STC*, p. 80).

Let us turn, now, from the director's approach to setting in the film to his approach to acting. What, then, is the role of the actor in the film's visual style? In line with his rejection of the "picturesque" in cinema, Kozintsev insisted that *Hamlet* be performed by individuals who somehow managed to avoid looking like actors in makeup (*STC*, p. 243). Kozintsev called for special attention to the faces and physical characteristics. It seems that the most extensive court scene in the film necessitated forty or fifty actors. Kozintsev remarked that "each person was selected as though he were to act a large part" (*STC*, p. 272). In this regard, Kozintsev's tactic was to stress the "isolated thing" over the "general quantity." Each detail—each fragment of the whole—was crucial. Kozintsev's special preoccupation with the face echoed, years later, the theoretical concerns of Bela Balazs, who had hailed the cinema's gift for revealing "the face of man." For Balazs, microphysiognomy and microdrama were essential components of the cinema. In Kozintsev's *Hamlet*, then, information is often conveyed through the face or the bodily gesture. Thus *Hamlet* manages not to be an excessively literary film, the pitfall of so many adaptations of classic texts.

In his quest for visual austerity, Kozintsev voiced the assurance that the audience would observe "not a touch of greasepaint" (*STC*, p. 264). Moreover, for Kozintsev, the bombastic acting style was to be avoided here. Elsewhere in the journal, the director of *Hamlet* notes that "bad actors 'embellish' the text and underscore the 'main' words, so that everything will get across" (*STC*, p. 272). Kozintsev proposes a more subtle, low-keyed approach, without embellishment. Notably, he remarks that "the job is to give a push to the audience, propelling it toward creativeness in order that it become a coauthor" (*STC*, p. 272). In Barthes's terms, then, Kozintsev calls for an audience that is a producer rather than a consumer of the text. Aesthetic components such as setting and acting must be manipulated to open rather than to close the text.

The Filmmaker as Archaeologist

Kozintsev's film version of *Hamlet*—like his later *King Lear*—does not seek to be a mere rendering of the play in question. Instead, the director works to expose new aesthetic possibilities. Kozintsev has evocatively compared his work on Shakespearean tragedy to the operations of the archaeologist. Both engage in

digging beneath the surface and in constructing a whole of some
sort from discovered fragments (*KL*, p. 49). But, as Kozintsev
notes, "the strange thing is that the deeper you dig, the more
contemporary everything that comes to the surface seems as it
reveals its significance." Thus, in the course of the contemporary
director's enterprise of retrieving the Shakespearean text, he
discovers something that is quite relevant to current concerns.
Here, again, Kozintsev engages in a meditation on the problem of
reading.

Kozintsev proposes to give us a Shakespeare who is truly "our
contemporary." This is not to suggest that Kozintsev operates
outside of the tradition of Shakespearean production. Alfred
Harbage, after all, has written that "no Shakespearean director
since Granville-Barker has displayed a fraction of this man's
general knowledge of literature and stage history."[7] What is
remarkable about Kozintsev is that, working within a tradition of
which he is conscious and knowledgeable, he manages to
discover a Shakespearean text that has something new to say.
That approach to Shakespeare which stresses the relevance of
his texts for the modern audience is forcefully represented in the
work of the Polish critic Jan Kott. We may usefully situate
Kozintsev's theory and practice in relation to Kott's volume
Shakespeare: Our Contemporary. Kott proposes a *Hamlet* that is
"enriched by being of our time." A double task faces the
director: to create a *Hamlet* that is at once faithful to
Shakespeare and contemporary, as well. It is not a "forced
topicality," which Kott is suggesting here. He is certainly not
calling for a production "set in a cellar of young existentialists."
Like Kozintsev, Kott seems primarily concerned with what the
former calls the "inner action." Noting that *Hamlet* has been
rendered in various kinds of costume, Kott observes that costume
is actually not very important. Instead, "what matters is that
through Shakespeare's text we ought to get at our own modern
experience, anxiety and sensibility."[8] Kozintsev's *Hamlet* and
King Lear attend to the "inner action," then, in order to get at
precisely this "modern experience" of which Kott speaks. Kott
evocatively observes that *"Hamlet* is like a sponge. Unless it is
produced in a stylized or antiquarian fashion, it immediately
absorbs all the problems of our time." Kozintsev's *Hamlet* is thus
no mere period piece or cultural ritual; it is vigorously and
intensely of its time. Kozintsev once remarked that modern dress

versions of *Hamlet* nevertheless concern themselves with a life
of the past. Thus, he proposed something different, a play
rendered in sixteenth century costume that yet managed to
achieve modernity (*STC*, p. 237).

Kozintsev seems to have conceived of the modernity of his
production intertextually in relation to Olivier's film version.
Recognizing what current criticism would call the plural text,
Kozintsev suggested the possibility of multiple readings. Therefore, although he admired the Olivier version, he sought to posit
yet another reading of the text. After viewing Olivier's film, he
felt quite encouraged in his plan to film *Hamlet.* Situating what
he wanted to do in relation to what Olivier had already done,
Kozintsev sought to produce meaning through difference.
Olivier, after all, had not treated a theme that would be a central
obsession of Kozintsev's—the theme of government (*STC*, p.
234). For Kozintsev, in fact, this theme had been "cut" by Olivier
in his interpretation.

In his journal, Kozintsev wrote that he was interested in the
play "mainly by its proportion and conformity with contemporary life" (*STC*, p. 237). For him, the play is "a tragedy of
conscience" (*STC*, p. 243). This last statement, perhaps, takes us
to the heart of Kozintsev's project in his adaptation of *Hamlet.*
Seizing precisely upon the theme of government, which he felt
Olivier to have "cut," Kozintsev retrieves a play that somehow
manages to reflect modern situations. As Antonin and Mira
Liehm have observed, Kozintsev's version of *Hamlet* takes up the
problem of the intellectual in society. Indeed, the society in
question here is corrupt and criminal. A focus of the play is upon
the manner in which the intellectual contrives to survive in that
society. This intellectual, the Liehms point out, is in search of
truth.[9] In this context, then, Hamlet's indecision, for instance,
takes on a new dimension. Does the film refer to the situation of
the intellectual in a modern version of such a repressive state? Is
this the "tragedy of conscience" to which Kozintsev refers in a
journal entry? Kozintsev's *Hamlet* is certainly suggestive in this
regard. In an essay on Shakespeare's play, Kozintsev notes in
Hamlet's encounter with the ghost "the noble theme of social
duty" (*STC*, p. 150). According to Kozintsev's interpretation of
the text, the ghost refers not to a sexual crime, but rather to the
throne's defamation. For Kozintsev, then, the ghost undertakes
to reveal to Hamlet "the destruction of the state, now ruled by an

incestuous murderer" (*STC*, p. 150). Kozintsev discovers in the Shakespearean text possibilities for rigorous political analysis. Even the setting of the play assumes a political signification for Kozintsev. Thus he writes: "The architecture of Elsinore does not consist in walls, but in the ears which the walls have. There are doors, the better to eavesdrop behind, windows, the better to spy from. The walls are made up of guards. Every sound gives birth to echoes, repercussions, whispers, rustling" (*STC*, p. 225). In Elsinore, perhaps, Kozintsev seizes upon elements which reflect the contemporary milieu. Recalling Kott's assertions, however, it must also be noted that Kozintsev's film version of *Hamlet* is not only up to date in interest, but faithful to Shakespeare as well. This duality is one of the film's special achievements.

The Way to the Interior

In his theoretical analysis of Shakespeare's soliloquies, Kozintsev reveals particular insights into the problems of literary structure. For Kozintsev, the soliloquies are often "whole scenes in code." The reader must labor to attempt to break the code, an enterprise which Kozintsev compares to that animated by the detective novel. The soliloquy, then, elicits an attempt on the part of the reader "to establish an entrance into the action." In describing this hermeneutic task, Kozintsev is, of course, thinking of the director as reader. Kozintsev remarks that various hypotheses are to be considered in the course of the search for "the main clue." Here, again, Kozintsev evinces a concern with the "inner action." In the intellectual quest that aims at breaking the code of the soliloquy, Kozintsev sees "the way to the interior, to the essence of the action, to the unfolding of the thought behind the whole tragedy" (*KL*, p. 34). It must be noted, however, that Kozintsev's strategy was not to isolate the soliloquy, thereby privileging it in relation to other sections of the text. Kozintsev's reading is dialectical in that meaning is produced in the dynamic interaction of textual moments. Kozintsev did not approve of those productions of Shakespeare, undertaken by certain travelling companies, in which the soliloquies were emphasized at the expense of other aspects of the plays. Instead, Kozintsev proposes a "life-like unity of continuous action, taking place on all planes at once" (*KL*, p. 38).

It must be stressed that Kozintsev's sense of the textual structures in question is marked by a predilection for conflict and collision. Here we may think of Mikhail Bakhtin's notion of the dialogical text, as posited in his study of Dostoevsky's poetics. In Bakhtin's dialogical text, no single voice dominates. Instead, different voices collide with each other, thereby radicalizing the text. Thus, when Kozintsev approaches Hamlet's first soliloquy, for instance, he situates it in relation to something else: "crowds of people hurrying to the carnival against a backdrop of noise and music and of faces flitting past" (*KL*, p. 39). Seizing upon what Siegfried Kracauer saw to be film's predilection for crowds—the so-called "flow of life"—Kozintsev devises a strategy here that manages to add great tension to the soliloquy. The approach may be described as dialogical because neither element really dominates. Like Bakhtin, Kozintsev is a radical reader. His filmic reading of *Hamlet* sets the text in motion. Indeed, for Kozintsev, "everything lies in living movement" (*KL*, p. 39).

Kozintsev's approach to the filming of Hamlet's famous "To be or not to be" soliloquy is instructive, for it reveals something about his cinematic tactics in general. The task before him here—the director has related—was not merely to locate some scene in which to place his speaker. Instead, Kozintsev labored "to reveal the link between the hero's spiritual life and the material world" (*KL*, p. 114). Several possible approaches were considered and rejected until a final one was at last settled upon. In the first possible approach explored by Kozintsev, Hamlet would be rendered making his way through a long corridor: "it was as if he were walking through life, the life in which it was better 'not to be' " (*KL*, p. 114). Sounds suggesting "the voices of life" entered into a dialogue with Hamlet's thoughts. These sounds included those of soldiers engaged in a drill and of students in a classroom. Kozintsev eventually discarded this possible approach because he felt that "it seemed like an illustration" (*KL*, p. 115). Other approaches were proposed. One, involving a path through a partially burning forest, was rejected on the grounds of being overly symbolic. Finally, Kozintsev settled upon a setting discovered on a sea shore in the Crimea: "The rocks formed huge blocks and in order to find our way to the sea we had to displace them and negotiate more piles of rocks. The camera followed behind Hamlet—the cold grey-black surfaces towered over him, and one impasse followed another." Without indulging in the intentional fallacy, it might be remarked that Kozintsev has succeeded quite admirably here in achieving what he set out to do in rendering this soliloquy. That is, he manages to link "the hero's spiritual life and the material world." Kozintsev's project in this regard might be described as a quest for what Eliot called the objective correlative, the formula for a particular emotion. Kozintsev, then, confronts the problem of the objective correlative cinematically. For him, "the whole point was to link the rhythm of the cine camera's movements with the main character's train of thought" (*KL*, p. 115). Thus, in his rendering of the soliloquy, Kozintsev achieves a poetic cinema. Cinematic technique is correlated with states of mind.

With dizzying speed, Kozintsev's *Hamlet* plunges us into the rhythm and tone of the young prince's world. A specter traces its outline over the surface of the water. A world on the edge of oblivion—a world articulated throughout the film by Kozintsev's manipulation of the frame—casts its shadow over our eyes. We are taken to the brink of an abyss, an unbroken expanse of water, with the shadow of an ominous and unknown world beyond. Rather than alleviating our fear by replacing this with a reverse shot of the castle, the outlines of the shadow are displaced by the coarse surface of stone. The camera moves across this ominous surface, but no legible shape is articulated. This is the cinematic space of the unknown and the unknowable. A horseman arrives from nowhere. He enters the now partially visible fortifications. A drawbridge encloses him—and us—in a space characterized by disorientation. No establishing shot proposes a plan or a provisional meaning for this space. The camera quickly follows the young prince within, thereby penetrating the unknown at breakneck speed. The ominous stones of Elsinore appear animate; they are made to live through the movement of actor and camera, as well as through rapid editing. Hamlet and his mother embrace; a black curtain drops across a towering window behind them, marking the prince's arrival. The building has come alive with Hamlet's presence.

The Ghost

The ghost represents a formidable problem to any director of *Hamlet*. How ought one to represent the ghost? In his journal,

Kozintsev reveals the rationale for the approach to the problem of the ghost that is taken in his film version. This approach needs to be investigated here, for Kozintsev's solution to the aesthetic problem is one of the film's most remarkable features. Kozintsev manages to create a ghost who somehow remains consummately hieratic. How does Kozintsev achieve this essential hieraticism? Kozintsev characterizes the ghost as "a poetic image, not a mystical one" (*STC*, p. 241). It is, then, precisely as such a "poetic image" that the director must seek to represent the ghost. For Kozintsev, "side-show movie miracles would be particularly vile: the transparent contours, double exposures to introduce an element of fear, and so on." Thus Kozintsev rules out what he calls "deviltry." As always, Kozintsev's great aesthetic tact enables him to avoid the *kitsch* effect. This problem of representation is especially challenging because the director constantly runs the risk of bad taste in depicting the ghost. It is partially in relation to this risk that Kozintsev's success in this regard is measured. Kozintsev argues that it is Hamlet alone who should be permitted to view his father's features in detail. The audience must be given a sense of the dead king's presence, a certain atmosphere, nothing more (*STC*, p. 242).

In his journal, Kozintsev suggests that perhaps for a moment the audience might be permitted to glance the ghost's sorrowful eyes, briefly visible from under his visor (*STC*, p. 242). The proposal suggests Kozintsev's acute sense of cinematic poetry. The hieratic exterior would reveal something else beneath— something strangely human—if only for an evanescent instant. Thus Kozintsev hints at the human dimension of the ghost, an important aspect of his interpretation. In the film, the ghost is played by a samba champion; the armour worn for the role necessitated an especially strong actor (*STC*, p. 200). Kozintsev traveled to the armory of the Hermitage in quest of some solution to the aesthetic problem of making the ghost concrete to the senses. Kozintsev alludes to his initial frustration when confronted by the problem. Anyone who has seen the film, of course, knows that he managed to solve it in magnificent fashion! In the relevant journal entry, Kozintsev describes his search through the Hermitage. Various objects were encountered in the quest—"helmets, breastplates, cuirasses"—without success, until Kozintsev finally managed to hit upon something that did indeed suggest the hoped-for solution. Kozintsev reports that he could not have invented such an object, so singular was it. What was the object? The director had hit upon a helmet stranded in a showcase in the Hermitage. It was the fact that the helmet's visor revealed "a face forged from steel" that so intrigued the director (*STC*, p. 264). In this face, Kozintsev read a particular signification: "some sort of proud suffering and ominous power." The interpretive operation at work here is especially interesting. The object encountered in the museum—a helmet dating from Nurenberg of the mid-sixteenth century—is seized upon in the artist's imagination, read, and thus pressed into the service of his project. Kozintsev goes on to interpret the implications of the fact that this physiognomy is made of steel, an essential contradiction: this, for the director, "communicated horror." Now Kozintsev describes the manner in which his imagination proceeded even further: "I immediately imagined a combination of two faces: the steel one, thrown back as though convulsed in pain, and behind it, appearing for an instant through the slits in the helmet when insulted love is mentioned, two eyes full of sorrow" (*STC*, p. 265). Thus the helmet served, in essence, as a catalyst for the director's imaginative reverie. The journal, of course, can only suggest the temporality of his perceptions before this object. Beginning with the object hit upon in the Hermitage, then, the artist proceeds first to interpretation of its contours, and then to a totally new imaginative conception which will be rendered concrete in the film. Thus Kozintsev's journal entries concerning his quest through the Hermitage provide a glimpse of the artist's chain of associations in the course of the process of creation.

Kozintsev deals with the aesthetic problem posed by the ghost in yet another fashion. In the ghost's early appearance on the ramparts, Hamlet is not the only one to see this visitor from beyond. Later, however, in his mother's chamber, Hamlet is alone in viewing the ghost's presence. Here, then, Kozintsev engages in a manipulation of off-screen space and its relation to that space within the frame of the screen. At this point, the ghost remains in off-screen space. We are made aware of the ghost's presence beyond the frame in two important ways. The hieratic music, heard during the ghost's earlier appearance, is heard again. We associate this music with the ghost's presence. Another way in which the ghost's presence is signified is through the play of expressions upon Hamlet's face. Here, Kozintsev utilizes the cinema's propensity for effects of microphysiognomy, as proposed by Balazs. The placement of the ghost in off-screen space solves another aesthetic problem confronted by Kozintsev at this point in the film. The ghost has already been shown earlier. Indeed, some of its crucial hieratic quality might be lost if the ghost were present in excess. Thus Kozintsev's tactic is to locate the ghost beyond the frame of the screen. Its image must now be reconstructed from memory. Unseen, its hieraticism is maintained.

Mirror Structure

Shakespeare's text involves a manipulation of frames in its famous play-within-the-play element. It has been pointed out by Lucien Dallenbach that the mirror structure—or *mise en abyme*—in *Hamlet* is of the simplest sort: the interior play is similar to the framing play, but not its exact duplicate. Such a strategy would produce the effect of an infinite regress such as one finds on a Quaker Oatmeal box, which appears to repeat itself infinitely within itself. Dallenbach notes that the interior play in *Hamlet* is a story of the prehistory of the play which contains it. It is the visualization of those events which took place before the play we watch. Moreover, for Dallenbach, the interior play suggests the future of the play that encloses it. The clash of reality and imagination is marked in the play-within-the-play sequence in Kozintsev's version by the torches which surround the interior stage, thereby serving as a frame within the frame of the screen. It is interesting to note that these torches repeat other torches seen at the beginning of the film, which also operated as a kind of frame. The tactic of repetition intensifies the frame-within-the-frame phenomenon. Kozintsev has revealed a special sensitivity to the possibilities for mirror structure in the play. At one point, it seems, the Polish director Andrzej Wajda gave to Kozintsev Stanislaw Wyspianski's text on *Hamlet*. Evidently, Wyspianski was fascinated by the notion that Hamlet held some book as he ambled through Elsinore. The identity of that book intrigued Wyspianski, who guessed it to have been Montaigne. Later, Kozintsev reports, Jan Kott also speculated about the identity of the volume Hamlet carries with him. For Kott, although a Hamlet of Shakespeare's day would indeed have been carrying Montaigne with him, today's equivalent might carry Sartre instead! Kozintsev proposes to join in this "game" of speculation about the identity of the mysterious book: "However strange it might have seemed, I thought that the author of the book he was holding was . . . William Shakespeare" (*KL*, p. 138). Like Kott's guess, Kozintsev's strikes us as particularly modern. The anecdote suggests, then, Kozintsev's decidedly modern approach to Shakespearean adaptation in the cinema, as evinced in his *Hamlet* and, later, in his *King Lear*.

6

King Lear

EXTREMELY SUCCESSFUL in the adaptation to the cinema of Shakespeare's *Hamlet,* Kozintsev next turned to another of the tragedies from the canon, *King Lear.* It would be the director's last film, a powerful conclusion to one of the great cinematic *oeuvres.* Audiences led to expect excellence in Shakespearean adaptation after a viewing of Kozintsev's *Hamlet* were not disappointed by *King Lear.* Like his film version of *Hamlet,* Kozintsev's cinematic *King Lear* had both its theatrical and critical precedents. The film was not an index of an initial encounter with the play, but, rather, of an extended relationship with its complexities. Kozintsev had directed *King Lear* at the Gorky Theater in 1941. Thus, Kozintsev had already tackled the problems of staging long before he undertook a film version. In addition, in his critical study *Shakespeare: Time and Conscience,* Kozintsev had set forth a detailed analysis of Shakespeare's text. By the time of the film version, then, Kozintsev had already engaged the play both practically and theoretically. It is a commonly accepted critical notion that the various texts of an author may be read as relating to and commenting upon one another. Indeed, a reading of one text by an author serves to illuminate some other text by him. A thematic study of a writer, painter, or filmmaker will probably discern the play of similarity and difference that cuts through the *oeuvre* in question. Often, certain thematic obsessions will be posited. It seems, then, that Kozintsev's multiple views of Shakespeare's *King Lear* operate in relation to each other. Kozintsev's final film is to be read not only in terms of the other films that constitute his cinematic oeuvre, but in terms of his other approaches to King Lear, critical and

119

theatrical. Thus Kozintsev appears to have thought in terms of a single "work," of which his theatrical, critical, and cinematic efforts were "versions." Each version was not self-contained; it alluded, intertextually, to other possibilities, other versions. The ideology of the work of art as finished, complete, finds itself called into question by this radical aesthetic approach. Having already "read" *King Lear* through the theatre and through literary criticism, Kozintsev could now approach the play with the special possibilities of the cinema in mind. The text is, then, a rewriting in terms of another, very different medium. The director explicitly desired to avoid forcing his material—the play itself—to become cinematic. Such coercion would imply a false solution to the aesthetic problem of adaptation. Thus, a passage was not merely "to be 'set up for the cinema' (broken down into long shots and close-ups and positioned in front of the lens, etc.)" (*KL*, p. 54). Kozintsev wanted a more subtle approach which would involve a discovery within the text itself of "seedlings of what can be developed into dynamic visual reality" (*KL*, p. 54). We may think, for instance, of the manner in which Eisenstein discerned cinematic elements in literary texts written long before the birth of cinema! In this view, the cinema is, perhaps, already adumbrated in literary works of past centuries. For Borges, we recall, a work of art creates its precursors. We may expand this dictum to suggest that an entire medium—the cinema—has, as well, created its precursors. In approaching Shakespeare's *King Lear*, then, Kozintsev's task is to retrieve that which is potentially cinematic in this text of centuries past.

The film will be a discovery—or, better yet, a recovery—of the classic text. Kozintsev stipulated that he wished to extract his basic material from the text itself. Indeed, for the director, additional invention was neither necessary nor desirable. As always, "gadgets" and merely gratuitous technical effects were to be scrupulously avoided. Here, too, the desire to lay bare the system of the text may be noted, as well as an essential respect for the material to be adapted. If, as Todorov suggests, a reading never quite reaches the text which is its object, it could be said that Kozintsev's film is one of a series of approaches. The text is an absence, never fully realized. In its place is another text, whether theatrical, critical, or cinematic.

The All-Embracing Thought

As might be expected with a complex artist such as Kozintsev, even the film did not exhaust his perceptions of *King Lear*. The activity of reading did not stop there. Thus Kozintsev undertook yet another approach to Shakespeare's text in the form of a diary that unfolded in the course of his work on the film version. In it, Kozintsev scrutinizes himself scrutinizing *King Lear*. In reflexive fashion, then, it considers his filmic effort intertextually in relation to his previous approaches to *King Lear*. Published as *King Lear: The Space of Tragedy*, the diary provides us with rare insight into the director's interplay with his material, both the initial classic literary text which he is adapting, and the components of the medium itself. As should be quite obvious indeed from the manner in which Kozintsev returned again and again to Shakespeare's *King Lear*, the text had lingered in his mind for some years. Thus the film, and the diary composed in conjunction with its genesis, reflect an ongoing relationship with *King Lear*. The film cannot be comprehended outside of the context provided by this temporal process of the director's evolving relationship to the work.

In the diary, Kozintsev specifically points out that filmmaking cannot simply be limited to the space of the studio. Indeed, it is not merely a question of teamwork with various specialists. Instead—and significantly—Kozintsev stresses what we may call the experiential aspect of the process: "It means living for several years under the persistent influence of Shakespeare's picture of life, which you see as yet only dimly, one feature at a time, but the main point is the 'All-embracing thought' (Dostoevsky)—which you take as the most important" (*KL*, p. 48). The film becomes a trace, not of some external reality, but of the artist's experience of Shakespeare's text. The experience, we are told, spans several years. The film, perhaps, crystallizes the encounter. Kozintsev emphasizes the gradual nature of the process; the Shakespearean text is assimilated piece by piece, never entirely. Shakespeare—presumably less a man than a body of texts—mediates between the self and the world. The world is viewed through the prism of the text. Kozintsev's film will involve a double-distancing; one text alludes to another which, in

Lionard Merzin as Edgar/Poor Tom leading K. Cebric in the role of his father, the blinded Gloucester in *King Lear*

turn, alludes to the world. Kozintsev appears to be as conscious of this extensive mediation as, say, Ezra Pound was in his encounter with Propertius. For Pound, Propertius offered a means of reading the world. So, too, Kozintsev appears to have submitted himself to the "all-embracing thought" embodied in the prior text. In the diary, Kozintsev fondly recalls his friend and colleague Tynianov's suggestion that, in the course of filmmaking, walks and conversations are times for conception and formulation. Kozintsev goes on to remark that it is when he is walking that he engages in formulating his conception of Shakespeare's tragedies: "I hold imaginary conversations with friends who are no longer living and with favorite authors" (*KL*, p. 44). Dialogue suggests a process, a working-over. Thus, in his walks, Kozintsev would consider the tragedies in relation to various ideas and other texts. His technique was, then, intertextual and dialogical in the best sense.

Antonin and Mira Liehm, in their study of East European film since 1945, *The Most Important Art*, scrutinize Kozintsev's *King Lear* in relation to other adaptations of classic literary texts realized in the Soviet Union since 1963 and argue that it is "the only truly autonomous film" of the group. Its special power and aesthetic interest is compared to that of Eisenstein's *Ivan the Terrible* and Tarkovsky's *Andrei Rublev*. Within the context of Kozintsev's own rich *oeuvre*, the Liehms situate *King Lear* as the "pinnacle" of the director's "exceptional trilogy of reflections about post-Stalinist Russia." The components of this trilogy are, of course, the three literary adaptations of Kozintsev's final phase, *Don Quixote, Hamlet*, and *King Lear*. In the last film, the Liehms propose, Kozintsev "turned Shakespeare's parable to face the present."[1] In this regard, Kozintsev is to be thought of in relation to such figures as Jan Kott and Peter Brook, who also discovered something quite modern in Shakespeare's *King Lear*. In a chapter called "King Lear or Endgame," in his volume *Shakespeare Our Contemporary*, Kott situates *King Lear* intertextually in relation to that modern master of the absurd, Samuel Beckett. It is a stunning juxtaposition indeed! Kott remarks that "it is odd how often the word 'Shakespearean' is uttered when one speaks about Brecht, Durrenmatt, or Beckett."[2] Significantly, Kott points out that the term "means something different in relation to each of them." A lesson of the intertextual critical approach is that a text's meanings are at once produced and potentially altered in terms of other texts. Jorge Luis Borges, for instance, delights in the juxtapositions that result when he randomly rearranges the books on his shelves. Kott's juxtapositions are, however, hardly random. Indeed, while Shakespeare is summoned to help us in the perception of something in the modern dramatists, they too permit us to discover something in Shakespeare, precisely his modernity.

Peter Brook

A remark of Peter Brook's—encountered in his theoretical volume *The Empty Space*—provides a penetrating critical insight along intertextual lines: "Shakespeare is a model of a theatre that contains Brecht and Beckett, but goes beyond both. Our need in the post-Brecht theatre is to find a way forwards, back to Shakespeare."[3] The assertion is strengthened by a rather startling paradox which is, perhaps, fundamentally Eliotic in its proposal of discovering the end in the beginning, the future in the past. This paradox about movement—can one move ahead by moving back?—calls into question certain fundamental assumptions about literary chronology. Here, perhaps, is that "ideal order" of art once posited by Eliot. Brook's remark suggests a synchronic rather than the more typical diachronic approach; that is, Shakespeare on the one hand and Brecht and Beckett on the other become, in essence, contemporaries, no longer divided by centuries. It is not at all surprising that Kozintsev and Brook deeply admired each other's work, for these are theoretical notions with which the former would be most at home.

Indeed, Kozintsev believed Brook to be "the most interesting director in Europe" (*STC*, p. 31). Shared concerns and even parallel projects animated a mutual admiration. It is quite interesting to note, for instance, that both directors staged productions of *Hamlet* and *King Lear* which aspired to take a modern look at the classic texts, to "make it new," as Pound would say. Kozintsev observed Brook's production of *King Lear* for the National Theatre—starring Paul Scofield—when it was mounted in Russia and recorded his special fascination with it in his journal. For the Russian director, "Brook had pared away all sentimentality from his production just as people kill bedbugs before moving into a new flat which was previously occupied by people with dirty habits" (*KL*, p. 23). Kozintsev's witty comparison suggests the manner in which Brook had prepared to make himself quite at home in Shakespeare's *King Lear*. The text would be scoured of certain previous associations, layers of meaning left behind by previous approaches. The image of paring away is a compliment indeed from a director who so strongly valued austerity. Obviously quite struck by the force of Brook's production, Kozintsev remarks upon the difficulty of characterizing with any precision Brook's interpretation of the play as evinced in his staging of it. Kozintsev, however, suggests some possibilities: "the tragedy of the meaninglessness of man's existence, the absurdity of history" (*KL*, p. 23). As might be expected at this juncture, the name of Beckett is mentioned, and Kozintsev observes that it is "no accident" that Brook and his commentators often allude to the modern writer.

Yet, in spite of its exploration of the meaningless and the absurd, Brook's production of *King Lear* somehow managed not to leave Kozintsev feeling oppressed. Fascinated by his response in this regard, Kozintsev decided to explore it further. Thus Kozintsev was able to determine that it was art itself which operated as the hero of Brook's production, wherein it won a "triumphant victory" (*KL*, p. 24). Here is the interpretation of the production proposed by Kozintsev: "As far as I was concerned Peter Brook and Paul Scofield were talking not so much about the powerlessness of man, but about the harmony of art" (*KL*, p. 24). In this production, then, Kozintsev discerns what he describes as "complete harmony." For Kozintsev, "even the emptiness of the cold iron surfaces reminded one of the warmth of life, of the continuing movement of art" (*KL*, p. 24). Viewing the production intertextually, Kozintsev thinks of such giants as Tatlin, Meyerhold, and Gordon Craig. Thus Brook's text is read in relation to other modern texts and their strategies. If, for Kozintsev, this production is, in essence, about art, it is because much modern art is self-referential in this regard. And, of course, it is as a director himself—indeed, a director concerned quite practically with the aesthetic problems posed by Shakespeare's *King Lear*—that Kozintsev scrutinizes Brook's enterprise.

It is particularly interesting to note that Kozintsev discovers in Brook's notion of a "rough theatre" an idea commensurate with his own activities as a youth during the *avant-garde* period of the 1920s. In *The Empty Space*, Brook speaks of "the theatre that's not in a theatre, the theatre on carts, on wagons, on trestles."[4]

Again, Brook proposes what is fundamentally a paradox; this time it is a theater that is not in a theatre. The paradox, of course, is founded upon wordplay. Kozintsev responds by recalling his own participation in "agit-sketches on lorries, platforms made out of planks set up in town squares, on railway wagons." These early experiences taught the young Kozintsev "to be revolted by grandiloquence" (*KL*, p. 101). The agit-sketches had indeed been instances of "the theatre that's not in a theatre" posited by Brook.

At one point, Brook and Kozintsev found themselves both aspiring to realize film versions of *King Lear*. As artists and friends who had previously shared various mutual preoccupations, the two directors now decided to exchange ideas about their respective projects and approaches. The fascinating dialogue that evolved between these kindred sensibilities is part of the prehistory of their films. Brook, Kozintsev reports in his journal, was especially engaged by the possibilities for achieving a "delocalization of space" in his film version of *King Lear* (*KL*, p. 25). This aspiration determined Brook's approach to the problem of adaptation. The signs of historical milieu were to be avoided. Brook, Kozintsev reports, discerned an essential dishonesty in those directors who strive for what they consider to be authenticity of setting and detail in their Shakespeare productions. Kozintsev shared Brook's fascination with the possible "delocalization of space." Thus Brook introduced Kozintsev to the French director Alain Resnais whose films aspire to contest realities of time and space. Resnais would provide an instructive case in this regard. Another director who stood as a model for Brook was Carl Dreyer. In an interesting letter to Kozintsev, Brook refers to the example of the masterful Danish director's *The Passion of Joan of Arc*, one of the truly great classics of the silent cinema. Brook turned to *The Passion of Joan of Arc* for its solution to the particular aesthetic problem that now confronted him: "Can we make a Shakespeare film closer to the manner of Dreyer's *Jeanne d'Arc*? I want to avoid background. How? To what degree? And you?" (*KL*, p. 25). This passage is of enormous interest for what it reveals to us of the tone of the theoretical give-and-take generated between Brook and Kozintsev. At once, Brook appears to be posing questions to himself and to his esteemed colleague. There is great generosity to be detected here in the recognition of a common labor in which the two artists are simultaneously engaged, the solution to the aesthetic problems posed by the adaptation of *King Lear* to the screen. Brook's mention of Dreyer's film is not surprising. Indeed, *The Passion of Joan of Arc* still strikes many viewers as a radical work of art, daring in its pictorial tactics. As Siegfried Kracauer has suggested, Dreyer's approach in the film aimed at displacing "emphasis from history proper to camera-reality."[5] It might be said that in Dreyer's film the proliferation of close-ups involves attention to the specificity of the medium. As Balazs has observed, the cinema alters the situation encountered in theater whereby "the spectator sees the enacted scene as a whole in space."[6] This "whole" is split asunder through the explicitly cinematic technique of the close-up. *The Passion of Joan of Arc*, then, creates its own reality through multiple close-ups, a world fragmented into multiple shots. Balazs stressed the manner in which the action upon which life and death depended was largely conveyed through close-ups permitting attention to microphysiognomy.[7] Thus, for the director who aspires to a "delocalization of space"—as Brook did—*The Passion of Joan of Arc* would be an obvious model. Following Dreyer, then, Brook proposes an emphasis upon the close-up as a cinematic strategy. As early as 1916, Hugo Munsterberg had demonstrated the manner in which this device suggests a psychological phenomenon; for Munsterberg, "the close-up has objectified in our world of perception our mental act of attention."[8] To delocalize space through the use of close-ups—as Brook proposes—would, then, be to pass into the realm of subjectivity.

Kozintsev's response to Brook's proposal is at once a confirmation of "the power of delocalized space on the screen" (*KL*, p. 26) and a rejection of the suggestion that Dreyer's approach be adopted. This response is absolutely crucial to us if we are to comprehend that approach outlined by Kozintsev for his own *King Lear* project. To examine these two artists—Brook and Kozintsev—is to define each in the play of similarity and difference. According to Kozintsev, then, "close-ups as the foundation of the action are often less effective in sound films than they were in the silents" (*KL*, p. 26). Thus Kozintsev shrewdly sets forth a reminder of the new aesthetic situation established by the sound film. Solutions to aesthetic problems of the sound cinema would be different from those of the silent cinema. For Kozintsev, "Dreyer's marvelous *Jeanne d'Arc* would have lost its strength if we had been able to listen to dialogue" (*KL*, p. 26). Thus, there is certainly no denial here of the power of the close-up. Indeed, Kozintsev recognizes its importance "when there is a need to look deep into the character's eyes, into the man's spiritual world" (*KL*, p. 26). In the sound film, however, the close-up simply cannot operate as the "foundation of the action." For Kozintsev, another approach must be sought.

Thus Kozintsev remarks that he thinks of "Shakespeare's text not only as a dialogue but as a landscape, notes from the author's diary, lines of verse, quotations" (*KL*, p. 26). Dialogue is to be displaced somewhat as the privileged node of interest. Other elements are to be pulled to the foreground in an attempt at an explicitly cinematic enterprise. It is well known that at the time of the inception of sound in the cinema, there was great fear among artists and intellectuals that filmmakers would now begin to grind out mere photographed theater and so-called "highly cultured dramas." Suddenly, the emphasis would be shifted from the visual to the verbal. Film would become a literary medium. Even today, anyone engaged, for instance, in the adaptation of Shakespearean plays to the screen runs the risk of creating such "highly cultured dramas." This would be to ignore the elements of film form, its ontology. Filmed theater so often tends to be a dismal affair, a mere transparent recording, with little or no attention to the specificity of the cinema. For Kozintsev, it would seem, a film which would take into account the properties of the medium would surely be more desirable. Recognizing the need for shifting interest somewhat from the dialogue in order to avoid photographed theatre, Kozintsev remarks upon strategies encountered in Brook's own theatrical enterprise: "This was beautifully expressed in your theatrical productions: the rhythm of the speech is the greatest influence, not always realistic but like the movement of sound" (*KL*, p. 26). This approach to sound, encountered in Brook, already suggests, perhaps, a cinematic strategy. For Kozintsev, Brook seizes upon the materiality of sound. A displacement of concern to its materiality would tend to defamiliarize dialogue. It ought to be mentioned here that Kracauer, in outlining the specificity of the cinema, suggests that one possible solution to the aesthetic problem posed by dialogue is a "shift of emphasis from the meanings of speech to its material qualities."[9] Kracauer deems such a shift to be essentially cinematic, a tactic for avoiding mere photographed theatre. After delineating that which he values in Brook's approach to sound in the aforementioned theatrical productions, Kozintsev turns to the cinema: "But how can the cinema help such expressiveness? Here the strength of the visuals outweighs the audible" (*KL*, p. 26). As in Kracauer, then, a stress upon the material characteristics of sound is related to a sense of the cinema as a visual medium. Thus Kozintsev describes to Brook his quest for "a visual *Lear*." In such a film, nature would operate in a manner analogous to that of a Greek chorus.

The critic Hugh Kenner has pondered the cinematic implications of Eliot's concept of the objective correlative.[10] Indeed, those people who were troubled by the possibility that, after the inception of sound, cinema would give way to "highly cultured dramas" were convinced of the idea that the medium ought to show rather than tell. Recognizing the quite obvious importance of the words that compose Shakespeare's texts, Kozintsev nevertheless argues that filmmakers ought to be concerned less with them than with "the circumstances in which they are spoken" (*KL*, p. 161). Here, Kozintsev discerns a fundamental difference between Shakespeare as produced in theater and in film. In his proposal, Kozintsev suggests the danger of filmed theater which places its emphasis upon verbal statements, and the significations they convey, as the means of advancing the story. In other words, Kozintsev firmly rejects those films which tell rather than show. Kracauer has pointed out the manner in which those films which emphasize dialogue in theatrical fashion also tend to deemphasize the role of inanimate nature.[11] A more cinematic approach would involve taking into account psychophysical correspondences, that is, the relations between the psychological and physical realms. In his diary, Kozintsev observes that the choice of location for filming *King Lear* was a complex enterprise: "We needed not a location for the action, but a world which would enter into the image of the character— sometimes the main character—and which would in many ways determine people's actions" (*KL*, p. 80). In Kozintsev's "visual *Lear*," then, inanimate nature—landscape, in particular—is emphasized.

Visual Tokens

Anyone who has seen Kozintsev's "visual *Lear*" will have been struck by the power of its landscapes. The choice of location involved absolutely crucial aesthetic decisions. What would be the precise spaces to animate the desired psychophysical correspondences? His quest for such scenes reveals a great deal about Kozintsev's approach. At one point, the director visited various English locales, which were quite naturally associated with Lear. It would seem obvious to take them into account. However, in scrutinizing appropriate castles, monuments, and a cathedral of the ninth century, Kozintsev felt that he had not yet discovered the space where the action of his film might unfold. Kozintsev's rejection of the choice of an English location for shooting would, perhaps, seem paradoxical outside of the context of his own theoretical approach, which suggests an essential neutralization of the details of time past. The director's project in his filmic enterprise was "to convince the audience of the actual existence of a world such as Lear's, which is not like prehistoric Britain (although who knows what it was like?), nor Shakespearean England, nor our century" (*KL*, p. 48). This is to stress the imaginary status of the world that unfolds in the play. The director's strategy of neutralization was appropriated because, for him, the world of Lear was "like all times" (*KL*, p. 48). Thus, in his journal, Kozintsev proposes that certain details, such as a mother breastfeeding her baby, or a beggar dressed in rags, are, in essence, the property of every century. In keeping with his taste for directorial austerity, Kozintsev suggests the necessity of first clarifying all details, and then removing "the archaeological and ethnographical, leaving only the most general features, making them visual tokens" (*KL*, p. 37). Thus, in shaping his cinematic material, in stripping away the inessential, the director's task is, in part, the creation of such "visual tokens." The world of the film is to be a world of signs.

The director has chronicled those "fantastic journeys"—those arduous treks through untamed terrain—undertaken in his quest for landscapes that might properly be characterized as "Shakespearean," that were to lead him to "the rocks of Kazantip" (*KL*, p. 132). His journal provides an index of

Kozintsev's delight at encountering at last the desired spaces. His quest set into play a reading of the landscape, an interpretation of its signs. In the course of his quest, while pausing at a spot marked by thorns and weeds, Kozintsev determined "that Edgar, the unfortunate outlaw, could have led his blind father here, and perhaps Lear and the Fool could also have wandered here after the storm" (*KL*, p. 128). As Kozintsev recognizes, the rationale for this decision is, ultimately, "inexplicable." Even so, he attempts to explore the process of association for us, and this reflexive exploration tells us something about the operations of the creative mind. Why does this particular space, then, animate the proper sensations, the necessary literary associations? Kozintsev alludes to "the fact that it was an expanse which was harsh, cruel and devoid of geographical features" (*KL*, p. 128). A chain of correspondences initiates the realization that this is "the land of tragedy." As might be expected, an untamed terrain, without roads or houses, posed practical problems of shooting. Such problems, however, were to be overcome. The locale was simply too perfect for the needs of Kozintsev's project! Artistic ideas might be realized now that the proper scene had presented itself.

Encountering this Shakespearean landscape suggested that the nonexistent world—hitherto only imagined—might be fabricated from multiple fragments. This is, of course, a fundamentally cinematic notion. In a sense, the imagined world was already there, albeit in scattered bits and pieces. Kozintsev describes an aspiration "to grasp its natural laws, to discover the links between the fragments, and to populate it with characters" (*KL*, p. 128). Echoing the theoretical insights of Kuleshov, Kozintsev suggests the manner in which montage technique might operate to create a new geography, a space of the mind. Seizing upon fragments of reality, film is to engender a new reality, thereby transcending the role of mere recording medium.

In seeking the proper fragments—not any would do—the procedure of trial and error was followed: "Catching sight of something in the distance which looked interesting and suitable we would race each other to the top, scrambling up steep paths and startling snakes and lizards, and would then discover that the likely place was no good at all, was not at all what we were after" (*KL*, p. 128). Kozintsev's encounter with the landscape before him involved a search for and a production of meaning. His response to the terrain needed to be keen, for, as he has written, "a film landscape is concealed, hidden under another sort of covering" (*KL*, p. 128). For Kozintsev, nature becomes a kind of book to be read, interpreted, deciphered. In the course of this reading, unexpected discoveries are made: "Ancient rocks are the earth's chronicle, history written with boulders and outcrops; each one has its own brand, the impression time has made upon it" (*KL*, p. 129). The mind of the artist plays with the landscape, rearranging its components, thereby creating new meanings. Kozintsev reports the discovery that the removal of certain rocks from a bit of land would cause the remaining ones to become "fragments of gravestones, an abandoned cemetery" (*KL*, p. 130). This process suggests the manner in which the physical world is transmuted by the power of imagination. For Kozintsev, the landscape presented "a reality which allowed one to invent, compose and imagine to the full extent of man's powers of fantasy" (*KL*, p. 130). In *King Lear*, then, fragments of landscape are assembled to constitute a system of signs. Kozintsev renders a landscape that oscillates between reality and fantasy. This oscillation accounts, in part, for the film's intensely poetic effect. The space covered by Lear and the Fool may, perhaps, be traced on old maps. But it is also an intensely symbolic space. As Kozintsev recognized, at times his landscape is quite clearly defined, while at other times it is vague, even oneiric.

Austere, spare, laconic, Kozintsev's film is strangely beautiful in its visual style. Excess and mannerism are rigorously avoided. The black-and-white photography of Jonas Gritsius is a major contribution to the film's distinctive look. The visual style of this *King Lear* operates to exile the merely unusual or beautiful. Indeed, the director's dictum throughout might have been an evocative line encountered in his journal: "There should be nothing to admire" (*KL*, p. 37). In a contemporary cinema that prides itself on pyrotechnics, such spareness functions as a marked element, deautomatizing our perceptions of the represented world.

The Carnivalistic

The film opens with the sound of a flute, and the titles written on

Yuri Yarvet as Lear and Valentina Shendrikova as Cordelia are reunited

the surface of a rough piece of tattered sackcloth, thereby setting a tone, a style. Everything here—as the director put it— will "be shot coarsely, sharply, spotlighting the roughness, the coarse-grained textures—sackcloth, rags, dark, weather-beaten faces" (*KL*, p. 85). As the titles unroll, there is the sound of the flute, only later identified as belonging to the Fool. Thus the film commences at that point to which it will return at its conclusion. Kozintsev gives his first and last word to the Fool. It is, perhaps, the Fool who speaks the truth. In a sense, it is his voice which dominates the film. As the song of the Fool continues, it is joined by the sound of stony soil crunching under unseen feet. These feet are joined by others, and then, finally, we have our first view of a complete human figure, a huddled, ragged child being pushed in a wheelbarrow. They proceed across the landscape, and the camera moves with them, thereby articulating the emptiness of the space. The film, then, begins with an anonymous journey to nowhere. Finally, however, the *telos* is reached, the castle at which we now see Kent and Gloucester speaking. It ought to be noted that in this first sequence we detect various allusions to the eccentric style, the obtrusive camera movement, the figure of a beggar without legs, a child in a wheelbarrow. Like the Fool, they may be described as carnivalistic elements whose resonance here is partially intertextual. Moreover, they adumbrate, perhaps, the film's carnivalistic strategy.

In Shakespeare's tragedy, Kozintsev has discovered the carnivalistic attitude toward power—its fundamental absurdity when subjected to the possibility of reversal. The film unfolds a world and its ruler: "And suddenly it all totters, collapses, falls apart and is destroyed" (*KL*, p. 32). Kozintsev's film posits a carnival of power, for in the course of this *King Lear* all will be subverted, all relations rendered ambiguous. This is a world in which King and Fool operate as doubles of one another, or even as aspects of a single self. Kozintsev has said that Lear can only become a heroic figure "when he understands that he is like any other man" (*KL*, p. 64). The remark suggests, perhaps, the exchange of roles that transpires in the carnival milieu.

In Kozintsev's film, the role of the Fool is intensified. As Yevgeniya Barteneva has pointed out, the jester is usually much older than the one played by Oleg Dal in Kozintsev's work, for

he "is still a boy, slim, with sad expressive eyes."[12] The figure of
the Fool is permitted to operate here in ways not indicated in
Shakespeare, suggesting Kozintsev's obsession with the techniques of carnivalism. The King enters without a fanfare, his
arrival indicated by the far-off noise of the Fool's bells, this
sound punctuated by silence. The essential interplay of King and
Fool is already posited. The director's journal reveals that the
Fool's bells possessed a personal note for Kozintsev, for whom
they operated "as a salute to FEKS" (*KL*, p. 119). The bells
operate, then, intertextually in rendering homage to the
director's youthful enterprise. Moreover, the bells strike a
subversive, carnivalistic voice which will cut through the
narrative as a whole. For Kozintsev, "the bell is a tongue stuck
out at pomposity and grandiloquence; a contempt for 'geometry'" (*KL*, p. 119). This subversive voice—it must be noted—
pertains not only to thematic matters, but to formal ones as well,
for it is precisely a contempt for "pomposity and grandiloquence" that we encounter in Kozintsev's approach to the
adaptation of Shakespeare to the screen.

In the carefully designed conjunction of Lear's appearance
and the sound of the Fool's bells, the director manipulates off-
screen space for added effect. The sources of sounds heard—the
aforementioned bells, as well as some laughter—remain
unknown, as they are situated off-screen. Figures on-screen look
beyond its frame in the direction of these unknown sources.
Then a glimpse of Lear is offered, but only the back of his head,
as the door opens in a shot which reveals quite another face, that
of the second figure within the frame, the Fool. Here, then,
pictorial composition is manipulated to produce thematic
meaning. As Lear turns at last, and the Fool moves out of view, it
seems that the King is now hidden behind the Fool's mask. This
turn of the action is especially evocative, suggesting a complex
play of shifting identities. Lear puts the mask aside, handing it
back to the Fool. This prelude already indicates the director's
fluid and creative approach to Shakespeare's text. Kozintsev's
reading brings the Fool to the foreground. Shifts in the text were
never merely the "whim" of the moment. Indeed, Kozintsev
reports an attempt through the making of the film to "listen
hard" to the "voices" of Shakespeare's characters. "Just you try

controlling them," Kozintsev writes about Shakespeare's characters (*KL*, p. 74).

Yuri Yarvet

An attentiveness to the demands of the text and its characters
was of great importance in the choice of Yuri Yarvet as the film's
Lear. In his choice of this actor, Kozintsev evinced his passion for
adhering to what he deemed to be the essence of Shakespeare's
text. Indeed, the task of locating an actor who was appropriate
for the role presented formidable problems to Kozintsev. The
director was for quite some time unhappy with the range of
actors scrutinized in the course of his search for a Lear. After
numerous screen tests had been undertaken, those around
Kozintsev began to urge him to hesitate no longer and to make a
selection. Why was the director rejecting the often first-rate
actors under consideration? Kozintsev, however, absolutely
insisted upon remaining faithful to his vision of Lear. Surely the
right actor for the role existed somewhere! For Kozintsev, the
screen tests did not yet reveal an actor who looked anything like
the Lear he envisioned in the mind's eye. It must be noted that
Kozintsev was not thinking merely in physical terms: "The ability
to become Lear," he wrote, "depends not on a similarity of
outward appearance but on a kinship of spiritual substance, the
constitution of the actor's inner world" (*KL*, p. 61). Intangible,
perhaps, this "kinship of spiritual substance" was the ingredient
Kozintsev needed now to make his film.

With costumes completed and the building of sets under way,
Kozintsev felt somewhat guilty about having gone ahead without
having discovered the actor who would play the central role in
the film. The director's decision to consider Yarvet for the part
appeared, to some, an odd one. Indeed, Yarvet spoke not Russian,
but Estonian! Surely this language barrier would be a major
drawback! Chosen to play another small role in the film, even
Yarvet doubted that he was being seriously considered as
Kozintsev's Lear. The director, however, was struck by Yarvet's
physiognomy. The actor's eyes, in particular, caught the
director's attention.

Thus Yarvet memorized a soliloquy from the text. Scrutinizing
Yarvet's screen test, Kozintsev realized that at last he had
discovered the actor he needed. The quest was over. Director

and actor were to enter into what would be an excellent working relationship. Kozintsev has remarked that he and Yarvet "loved the same qualities in Lear" (*KL*, p. 77). In spite of the fact that the director was opposed to dubbing in film, it was decided that, due to Yarvet's participation, *King Lear* would have to be dubbed. Yarvet's resemblance to the Lear Kozintsev imagined made dubbing worth the aesthetic gamble. Thus an Estonian text was prepared for Yarvet's use. To Kozintsev's delighted surprise, however, Yarvet rejected the decision to dub, after finding the dubbing script to be "revolting and unpoetic." (*KL*, p. 77). Yarvet registered his artistic determination to speak the words of Pasternak's Russian translation of Shakespeare in his own voice.

With the discovery of an appropriate actor to play Lear, Kozintsev set forth to make one of the truly great adaptations of Shakespeare in the history of the cinema. Kozintsev's *King Lear* is a testament to its director's artistic vision. In its foregrounding of the role of the Fool, Kozintsev's film alludes, interestingly, to a much earlier phase in the director's *oeuvre*, suggesting that that *oeuvre* may in fact be read as a structure.

7

Epilogue

"IN MY END is my beginning," the poet T. S. Eliot wrote in the great work of his final phase, *Four Quartets*. Indeed, the line might provide a fitting epigraph for a study of the *oeuvre* of Grigori Kozintsev. The culmination—the "end"—of Kozintsev's career is, of course, his quite majestic adaptation of Shakespeare's tragedy *King Lear*. In a way, though, this final film may also be said to contain the director's "beginning"—or at least something of it. Fragments of an earlier style—traces of his youthful concerns—are to be discovered embedded in this last great work of the director.

To be sure, the overall style of *King Lear* is decidedly different from the *avant-garde* style of the 1920s, when the young Kozintsev directed plays and films in collaboration with another very young man, Leonid Trauberg. But in *King Lear*--the conclusion of the director's final phase—the intertextual concern is there all the same. It may be discerned, for instance, in the "roughness" that dominates the pictorial compositions; and, especially, in the person of the Fool, whose foregrounded presence in the film evokes the "carnivalistic attitude" of the director's *avant-garde* years in the 1920s, decades before. Scrutinizing this film of the 1970s, we find it to be superimposed, as it were, upon films of the 1920s. The frame of the individual work of art breaks down somewhat, in order that other, earlier works may enter the picture. To watch the film is, then, to play a game involving absence and presence; the text—present before us—suggests other absent texts. The game necessitates that we be aware of those earlier films—their styles and concerns—so that we may comprehend the intertextual stance of the later text.

137

Kozintsev during the shooting of King Lear

Late novels by such modern (postmodern?) writers as
Vladimir Nabokov or John Barth often allude intertextually to
characters and situations in earlier works by the author. Such
allusions, of course, would make little sense to someone who had
not read the earlier texts. This reflexivity suggests that we read
all of Nabokov's or Barth's texts as a single text, the whole being
greater than the sum of its parts. Kozintsev's intertextual strategy
in *King Lear* suggests a similar approach. The director's strategy
in this regard is, however, more difficult to discern than
Nabokov's or Barth's. Thus we may say that in Kozintsev's *King
Lear*—strikingly modern as it may be—intertextuality is
naturalized, as it were. That is, intertextual elements are fully
integrated into the world of the fiction. The Fool plays his role in
the film's diegesis—albeit a subversive role, of course. The
moment in some reflexive art—whether in Nabokov or Barth—
when the fiction is clearly revealed for the artifice it is never
quite occurs in Kozintsev's *King Lear*, or in any of the three
works of the final phase, for that matter. Or—perhaps more
accurately—it does not *seem* to occur. The play unrolls to its
conclusion, with no substantial fractures in the diegesis, as there
would be in a film by, say, Godard.

Yet in this *King Lear* we can have it both ways. Indeed, the
carnivalistic subversion animated by the Fool in this remarkable
production may even operate to subvert the text in which he
finds himself, a Nabokovian situation indeed. This alternate
reading—quite different from the more usual reading, which
regards the film as "naturalistic"—is supported by the fact that
the Fool—among other elements—functions intertextually, in
calling attention to earlier concerns and styles. In other words,
the presence of the Fool makes us think about other films of the
director, thereby laying bare the filmic status of the world in
which he operates. We begin to think about Kozintsev's *oeuvre*
as a whole—less as a career, perhaps, than as a structure.
Suddenly, texts at the extreme poles of the director's career
appear to interpenetrate. We find ourselves measuring degrees
of similarity and difference. The diachronic gives way, then, to
the synchronic. As T. S. Eliot suggests in his poem, the beginning
is in the end.

We know that the director's "beginning" was also to have been
reflected in his final project, unrealized at the time of his death.
At the end of his career, Kozintsev planned to make a film which

would have been based on materials drawn from Gogol. The choice is significant. This last project—"Gogoliana"—evokes earlier intertextual encounters between Kozintsev and Gogol. We may think of the 1922 FEKS production of Gogol's *Marriage*, which the audacious young men entitled *A Gag in Three Acts: The Electrification of Gogol.* Or we may think of Kozintsev and Trauberg's film *The Cloak*, yet another reading of Gogol. Thus a thread is woven through the *oeuvre*, a series of encounters with Gogol, whom, we recall, Kozintsev and his friends thought of as "the most 'left' man in art." Thus the projected return to Gogol for material may be read as emblematic of a radicalism sustained. The decision suggests not just a rereading of Gogol's work, but a rereading of Kozintsev's, as well. The *oeuvre* would seem to fold back upon itself. But the director's final phase goes beyond mere repetition. This is not just nostalgia, a desire for time past.

"Does any influence of FEKS survive today?" an older Kozintsev asked. The powerful films of the final phase—*Don Quixote, Hamlet,* and *King Lear*—suggest a response to this question. "Generally speaking," Kozintsev remarked, "I think that in art there are certain periods which only bear fruit after many years." This is, perhaps, to suggest the impulse that animates the reflexive intertextuality of the director's last three works. It is very moving indeed when we discover elements of the *avant-garde* period of the 1920s—presumably extinguished by the repressions of Stalinism and its aesthetic of Socialist Realism—come alive once more in *Don Quixote, Hamlet,* or *King Lear.* The *avant-garde* elements—the carnivalism, the "roughness," the reflexivity—are, of course, refracted through the prism of time and memory. Nothing ever remains quite the same.

We know that a work of art means different things at different times; so do aesthetic devices. Indeed, the carnivalism of Kozintsev's final phase is especially striking against the background of Socialist Realism, with its ethic of stasis and order. For Kozintsev, "time can never exactly repeat itself. If what is revived today from the art of the 1920s were exactly like it was before, we would certainly question the usefulness of such regression: epigones are uninteresting." Thus, although the "beginning" is indeed in the "end," it is altered, reworked. There is, as Harold Rosenberg has suggested, a "tradition of the new," and one of the touchstones of that "tradition" is Soviet *avant-garde* art of the 1920s. Vital as that "tradition" is, however,

Kozintsev's final films are not content to recapitulate it. As Kozintsev wrote, "in any period man must remain faithful to his own time and to himself. It is bad for someone of sixteen to live as if he were fifty. The greatest happiness is to live at sixteen with all that those sixteen years signify, not to be older than one's age. And it is equally bad for an older man to try to remain what he was in his youth: to do that is not to be rejuvenated, but to fall back into childishness."[1] The carnivalism encountered in the films of the director's final phase is at once similar to and different from that of the 1920s. If there is repetition—the past recaptured—it is with a difference.

Much additional study of Kozintsev's work in the cinema is, of course, necessary if we are to begin to comprehend the evolution of Soviet film. In order to facilitate the work of young scholars, the increased availability of the director's films, as well as additional translation of his writings, would be most helpful next steps.

Notes and References

Chapter One

1. Grigori Kozintsev, "A Child of the Revolution," in Luda and Jean Schnitzer, eds., *Cinema in Revolution* (New York, 1973), p. 91.
2. Ibid., p. 92.
3. Ibid., p. 93.
4. Ibid., p. 94.
5. Ibid.
6. Ibid., p. 97.
7. Ibid.
8. Sergei Gerassimov, "Out of the Factory of the Eccentric Actor," in Schnitzer, p. 111.
9. Antonin and Mira Liehm, *The Most Important Art* (Berkeley, 1977), p. 56.

Chapter Two

1. (Norfolk, 1959), p. 30.
2. John Berger, *Art and Revolution* (London, 1969), p. 37.
3. *The Philosophy of Surrealism* (Ann Arbor, 1969), p. 68.
4. (Ann Arbor, 1973), p. 101.
5. Ibid.
6. Kozintsev quoted in *Sight and Sound* 3 (1973): 150.
7. Sergei Gerassimov, "Out of the Factory of the Eccentric Actor," in Schnitzer, p. 112.
8. Gerassimov, p. 115.
9. Victor Shklovsky, in Lee Lemon and Marion Reis, eds., *Russian Formalist Criticism* (Lincoln, Nebraska, 1965), p. 118.
10. *"La Nouvelle Babylone:* La Quantité se transforme en qualité," in *La Nouvelle Babylone* (Paris, n.d.), pp. 119-25.
11. Bakhtin, p. 101.
12. *King Lear: The Space of Tragedy* (Berkeley, 1977), p. 189.

13. Shklovsky, "Art as Technique," in Lemon and Reis, p. 12.
14. Museum of Modern Art Program Notes, November 1975.
15. *King Lear: The Space of Tragedy*, p. 163.
16. In Schnitzer, p. 100.
17. *Third Factory* (Ann Arbor, 1977), p. 55.
18. Ibid.
19. In Schnitzer, p. 101.
20. Yon Barna, *Eisenstein* (Bloomington, 1973), p. 59.
21. Quoted in Jay Leyda, *Kino* (London, 1960), p. 180.
22. In Schnitzer, p. 106.
23. Ibid., p. 108.
24. Gerassimov, p. 114.
25. Ibid., p. 115.
26. "FEKS, Grigori Kozintsev, Leonid Trauberg," in *La Nouvelle Babylone*, p. 35.
27. *King Lear: The Space of Tragedy*, p. 189.
28. Bakhtin, p. 105.
29. "La fin des années vingt," *Cahiers du Cinema* 230 (July 1971): 4-14.
30. "La fin des années vingt," p. 6.
31. "Socialist Realism in the Art of Cinema," in *Socialist Realism in Literature and Art* (Moscow, 1971), pp. 205-206.

Chapter Three

1. (Boston, 1970), p. 25.
2. Ibid., p. 27.
3. *The Icon and the Axe* (New York, 1968), p. 535.
4. "Soviet Literature," in *Problems of Soviet Literature* (Moscow, n.d.), p. 65.
5. *Discovering the Present* (Chicago, 1973), p. 15.
6. Ibid., p. 12.
7. Quoted in Marc Slonim, *Soviet Russian Literature* (London, 1969), pp. 160-61.
8. Billington, p. 535.
9. *Elements of Semiology* (Boston, 1970), pp. 28-30.
10. *S/Z* (Boston, 1974), p. 100.
11. *Soviet Marxism* (New York, 1961), p. 114.
12. Quoted in Mario Verdone and Barthélemy Amengual, *La FEKS* (Paris, 1970), p. 24.
13. *Theory of the Film* (New York, 1970), p. 60.
14. Ibid., p. 54.
15. *S/Z*, p. 76.
16. Ibid., p. 181.
17. Ibid., p. 52.

18. George S. Counts and Nucia Lodge, *The Country of the Blind* (Boston, 1949), pp. 128–29.

Chapter Four

1. *The Poet as Filmmaker* (Cambridge, 1973), p. 126.
2. Jay Leyda, *Kino* (London, 1960), p. 399.
3. Antonin and Mira Liehm, *The Most Important Art* (Berkeley, 1977), pp. 70–71.
4. Ibid., pp. 202–203.
5. *Sight and Sound* 28 (1959): 158.
6. Liehm, p. 316.
7. *Problems of Dostoevsky's Poetics* (Ann Arbor, 1973), p. 110.
8. Ibid.
9. *Rabelais and His World* (Cambridge, 1968), p. 275.
10. Ibid., pp. 19–20.
11. *Sade/Fourier/Loyola* (New York, 1976), pp. 88–89.
12. *Problems of Dostoevsky's Poetics*, p. 109.
13. "Homo Ludens Revisited," *Yale French Studies* 41 (1969): 56.
14. "The Oasis of Happiness: Toward an Ontology of Play," *Yale French Studies* 41 (1969): 23.
15. Ibid., pp. 24–25.

Chapter Five

1. *Shakespeare: Time and Conscience* (New York, 1966). Page references are indicated in the text by the abbreviation (*STC*).
2. (Ann Arbor, 1977), p. 56.
3. *The Young Tolstoi* (Ann Arbor, 1972), p. 8.
4. *The Poetics of Prose* (Ithaca, 1977), pp. 234–46.
5. *The Icon and the Axe*, p. 577.
6. *Ezra Pound and Sextus Propertius* (Austin, 1964), p. 19.
7. "The Bard as Mankind," *New York Times*, August 7, 1976, p. 4.
8. *Shakespeare Our Contemporary* (New York, 1974), pp. 58–59.
9. *The Most Important Art*, p. 316.

Chapter Six

1. *The Most Important Art*, p. 316.
2. *Shakespeare Our Contemporary*, p. 131.
3. *The Empty Space* (New York, 1978), p. 86.
4. Ibid., p. 65.
5. *Theory of Film* (New York, 1970), p. 79.
6. *Theory of Film* (New York, 1970), p. 30.
7. Ibid., p. 74.

8. *The Film: A Psychological Study* (New York, 1970), p. 38.
9. *Theory of Film*, p. 109.
10. *A Homemade World* (New York, 1975), p. 126.
11. *Theory of Film*, p. 104.
12. *"One Day with King Lear,"* *Soviet Film* 9 (1969): 6.

Chapter Seven

1. Grigori Kozintsev, "A Child of the Revolution," p. 105.

Selected Bibliography

Primary Sources

"A Child of the Revolution," in Luda and Jean Schnitzer, eds., *Cinema in Revolution*. New York: Hill and Wang, 1973.
King Lear: The Space of Tragedy. Berkeley: University of California Press, 1977. (Abbreviated *KL* throughout text.)
Shakespeare: Time and Conscience. New York: Hill and Wang, 1966. (Abbreviated *STC* throughout the text.)

Secondary Sources

AUMONT, JACQUES, et al. "La metaphore 'commune,'" *Cahiers du Cinema* 230 (July 1971): 43–51. An incisive French analysis of *The New Babylon*.
BARNA, YON. *Eisenstein*. Bloomington: University of Indiana Press, 1973. This comprehensive study of Eisenstein alludes interestingly to his artistic encounter with Kozintsev.
BARTENEVA, YEVGENIYA. "One Day with *King Lear*," *Soviet Film* 9 (1969): 6. The author chronicles the activity on the set of Kozintsev's last film.
BILLINGTON, JAMES. *The Icon and the Axe*. New York, Knopf, 1968. This cultural and intellectual history of post- and prerevolutionary Russia usefully alludes to Kozintsev's conception of *Don Quixote* and *Hamlet*.
BROOK, PETER. *The Empty Space*. New York: Atheneum, 1978. This theoretical volume is important for the student of Kozintsev who will want to analyze points of contact and divergences between the two director-theoreticians.
ECKERT, CHARLES, ed. *Focus on Shakespearean Films*. Englewood Cliffs, N.J.: Prentice-Hall, 1972. This anthology includes essays on Kozintsev's *Hamlet* by Michael Kustow, Dwight Macdonald, and Eric Rhode.

145

FERGUSON, OTIS. *The Film Criticism of Otis Ferguson.* Philadelphia: Temple University Press, 1971. Ferguson comments on Kozintsev and Trauberg's *The Youth of Maxim.*

FRANCE, ANNA KAY. *Boris Pasternak's Translations of Shakespeare.* Berkeley: University of California Press, 1978. In his Shakespeare films, Kosintsev used Pasternak's translations of *Hamlet* and *King Lear.* This study considers in detail Pasternak's strategies of creative translation. For Pasternak, translation was itself an artistic enterprise.

KOTT, JAN. *Shakespeare Our Contemporary.* New York: Norton, 1974. Kott discovers in Shakespeare's *oeuvre* texts relevant to modern man. Kott's methodology is useful for the student of Kozintsev's *Hamlet* and *King Lear.*

LEYDA, JAY. *Kino.* London: George Allen and Unwin, Ltd., 1960. This extensive historical survey of Soviet cinema takes into account the work of Kozintsev and Trauberg.

LIEHM, ANTONIN and MIRA. *The Most Important Art.* Berkeley: University of California Press, 1977. This comprehensive examination of East European film since 1945 makes a number of shrewd remarks on Kozintsev's final phase.

NARBONI, JEAN, and OUDART, JEAN-PIERRE. *"La Nouvelle Babylone* (La metaphore 'commune' 2),*" Cahiers du Cinema* 232 (October 1971): 43–51. A continuation of the analysis of *The New Babylon* undertaken in No. 230.

La Nouvelle Babylone. Paris: Dramaturgie, n.d. An invaluable French anthology of texts on FEKS by Bernard Eisenschitz, Vladimir Nedobrovo, Victor Shklovsky, Yuri Tynianov, and others.

RAPISARDA, GIUSI, ed. *La Feks: Kozincev e Trauberg.* Rome: Officina Edizioni. An Italian anthology of texts on FEKS, including both primary and secondary sources.

RHODE, ERIC. *A History of the Cinema.* London: Allen Lane, 1976. The films of Kozintsev and Trauberg are mentioned in the context of a more general historical survey.

ROBINSON, DAVID. *The History of World Cinema.* New York: Stein and Day, 1973. The films of Kozintsev and Trauberg are mentioned in the course of a more general historical survey.

SCHNITZER, LUDA and JEAN, eds. *Cinema in Revolution.* New York: Hill and Wang, 1973. A superbly lively collage of texts by the luminaries of the Soviet cinema, including Gerassimov, Kozintsev, and Yutkevitch.

VERDONE, MARIO, and AMENGUAL, BARTHELEMY. *La Feks.* Paris: Premier Plan, 1970. An excellent account of the *avant-garde* enterprise of Kozintsev and Trauberg, the volume includes interviews and other documents.

Filmography

(For the convenience of English-language readers, titles of the films that Kozintsev directed appear here, where an English version exists, first in English translation. The original Russian title follows, transliterated into the Roman alphabet. For information about rental of Kozintsev's films subtitled in English see the note at the end of this section.)

THE ADVENTURES OF OCTYABRINA [POKHOZDENIYA OKTYABRINI] (Sevzapkino & Feks, 1924)
Codirector: Leonid Trauberg
Assistant Director: G. Rappoport
Screenplay: Kozintsev and Trauberg
Photography: F. Verigo-Darovski, Ivan Frolov
Artistic Director: B. Tchaikovski
Set Designer: Vladimir Yegorov
Cast: Z. Tarkhovskaya, Sergei Martinson, E. Koumeiko, A. Tserep, F. Knorre, E. Kiakcht, N. Boiarinov, Piatnitski, G. Rappoport, D. Fichov, D. Milovzorov, V. Landa
Running time: 3 reels, 980 meters (approximately 42 minutes)

MISHKA AGAINST YUDENITCH [MICHKI PROTIV YOUDENITSA] (Sevzapkino, 1925)
Codirector: Leonid Trauberg
Scenario: Kozintsev and Trauberg with I. Koukina
Photography: F. Verigo-Darovski
Production Designer; Yevgeni Enei
Cast: Choura Zavialov, P. Pona, S. Gerasimov, A. Kostrichkin, E. Koumeiko, E. Gal, A. Alexandrov, T. Ventsel, I. Jeimo
Running time: 2 reels, 680 meters (approximately 29 minutes)

THE DEVIL'S WHEEL [CHYORTOVO KOLESO] (Leningradkino, 1926)
Codirector: Leonid Trauberg
Assistant Directors: M. Geraltovski, S. Chkliarevski
Scenario: (from a story by Kaverin), Andrei Piotrovski
Photography: Andrei Moskvin
Production Designer: Yevgeni Enei
Cast: Ludmila Semyonova, N. Foregger, Pyotr Sobolevski, Sergei
    Gerasimov, Emil Gal, A. Tserep, N. Gododnitchi, V. Lande, S.
    Martinson, E. Koumeiko, I. Berzine, I. Jeimo, A. Kostrichkin, V.
    Plotnikov, A Kostomolotski, A. Arnold, A. Kapler
Running time: 7 reels, 2,600 meters (approximately 112 minutes)
16mm. rental: Macmillan/Audio-Brandon

THE CLOAK [SHINEL] (Leningradkino, 1926)
Codirector: Leonid Trauberg
Assistant Director: I. Chpis
Scenario: (from two Gogol stories, "The Cloak" and "Nevski
    Prospect"), Yuri Tinyanov
Photography: Andrei Moskvin, Yevgeni Mikhailov
Production Designer: Yevgeni Enei
Cast: Andrei Kostrichkin, Sergei Gerasimov, Anna Zheimo, A.
    Eremeiva, A. Kapler, Emil Gal, V. Plotnikov, Pyotr Sobolevski
Running time: 7 reels, 1,920 meters (approximately 82 minutes)
16mm. rental: Macmillan/Audio-Brandon

LITTLE BROTHER [BRATICHKA] (Sovkino, Leningrad, 1927)
Codirector: Leonid Trauberg
Assistant Director: I. Chpis
Scenario: Kozintsev and Trauberg
Photography: Andrei Moskvin
Production Designer: Yevgeni Enei
Cast: P. Sobolevski, I. Jeimo, V. Plotnikov, S. Martinson, S. Gerasimov,
    T. Gourietskaya
Running time: 6 reels, 1,584 meters (approximately 67 minutes)

**S.V.D. (THE CLUB OF THE BIG DEED) [SOYOUZ VELIKOGO
DELA]** (Sovkino, Leningrad, 1927)
Codirector: Leonid Trauberg
Assistant Director: I. Chpis
Scenario: Yuri Tinyanov, Yuri Oxman
Photography: Andrei Moskvin
Production Designer: Yevgeni Enei

Cast: Pyotr Sobolevski, Sergei Gerasimov, Sophie Magarill, Andrei
Kostrichkin, K. Koklov, I. Jeimo, M. Michel, Bronchtein, V.
Fedosiev, Le Semenova, N. Mitchourine
Running time: 6 reels, 2,100 meters (approximately 89 minutes)

THE NEW BABYLON [NOVYI VAVILON] (Sovkino, Leningrad, 1929)
Codirector: Leonid Trauberg
Assistant Directors: Sergei Gerasimov, S. Bartenev
Photography: Andrei Moskvin, Yevgeni Mikhailov
Production Designer: Yevgeni Enei
Music (for performance with film): Dmitri Shostakovich
Historical Advisor: A. Molok
Cast: Yelena Kuziman, Pyotr Sobolevski, D. Gutman, Sophie Magarill,
S. Gerasimov, Andrei Kostrichkin, S. Goussev, I. Jeimo, A.
Glouchkova, E. Tcherviakov, A. Zarjiskaya, V. Poudovkin, A.
Arnold, O. Jakov, L. Semenova
Running time: 8 reels, 2,200 meters, (approximately 93 minutes)
New York premiere: December 1929 at the Cameo Theater [A Times
Square house specializing in Soviet films]
16mm. rental: Not available at present

ALONE [ODNA] (Soyuzkino, Leningrad, 1931)
Codirector: Leonid Trauberg
Scenario: Kozintsev and Trauberg
Photography: Andrei Moskvin
Production Designer: Yevgeni Enei
Sound Director: Leo Arnstam
Sound Operator: I. Volk
Music: Dmitri Shostakovich
Cast: Yelena Kuzmina, Pyotr Sobolevski, Sergei Gerasimov, M.
Babanova, Van Liu Siana, I. Jeimo, B. Tchirkov
Running time: 7 reels, 2,200 meters (approximately 93 minutes)
New York premiere: May 1932 at the Cameo

THE YOUTH OF MAXIM [YUNOST MAKSIMA] (Lenfilm, 1935)
Codirector: Leonid Trauberg
Assistant Directors: N. Kocheverova, K. Lokchina, M. Nesterov
Scenario: Kozintsev and Trauberg
Photography: Andrei Moskvin
Sound Operator: I. Volk
Music: Dmitri Shoskakovich
Cast: Boris Chirkov, Stepan Kayukov, Valentina Kibardina, Mikhail

Tarkhanov, M. Chelkovski, S. Leontiev, P. Volkov, B. Blinov, V.
   Sladkopevtsev
Running time: 9 reels, 2,678 meters (85 minutes)
New York premiere: April 1935 at the Cameo
16mm. rental: Macmillan/Audio-Brandon

THE RETURN OF MAXIM [VOZVRASHCHENIYE MAKSIMA]
(Lenfilm, 1937)
Codirector: Leonid Trauberg
Assistant Directors: N. Kocheverova, I. Fraz, V. Soukoboko, M.
   Gueraltovski, A. Gourvitch
Scenario: Kozintsev and Trauberg
Photography: Andrei Moskvin
Production Designer: Yevgeni Enei
Sound Operators: I. Volk, G. Koutorianski
Music: Dmitri Shostakovich
Cast: Boris Chirkov, Valentina Kibardina, Alexander Zrazhevski, A.
   Kuznetsov, Mikhail Zharov, Vasili Vanin, A Chistyakov
Running time: 12 reels, 3,082 meters (98 minutes)
New York premiere: November 1937 at the Cameo
Not currently available for rental

THE VYBORG SIDE (Released in the U.S.A. as NEW HORIZONS)
[VYBORGSKAYA STORONA] (Lenfilm, 1939)
Codirector: Leonid Trauberg
Scenario: Kozintsev and Trauberg
Photography: Andrei Moskvin, G. Filatov
Production Designer: V. Vlasov
Sound Operators: I. Volk, G. Koutorianski
Music: Dmitri Shostakovich
Cast: Boris Chirkov, Valentina Kibardina, Natalia Uzhvi, Mikhail
   Zharov, A. Christyakov, Yuri Tolubeyev, Maxim Strauch, Mikhail
   Gelovani
Running time: 12 reels, 3,276 meters (103 minutes)
New York premiere: May 1939 at the Cameo
Not currently available for rental

"Incident at the Telegraph Office" in FIGHTING FILM ALBUMS
   Number 2 (1941) (Also known as FILM NOTES ON BATTLES
   Number 1 and 2)
Not known to have been released in the United States; no further infor-
mation available.

SIMPLE PEOPLE (also called **PLAIN PEOPLE**) **[PROSTIYE LYUDI]** (Lenfilm, 1945, suppressed; released August 1956 in a reedited version)
Codirector: Leonid Trauberg
Scenario: Kozintsev and Trauberg
Photography: Andrei Moskvin, A. Nazarov
Production Design: Yevgeni Enei, D. Vinitski
Editing: V. Mironova
Sound: I. Volk
Music: Dmitri Shostakovich
Cast: Yuri Tolubeyev, Boris Zhukovski, Yelena Korchagina-Alexandrovskaya, O. Lebzak, F. Babadzhanov, I. Koudriavtseva
Running time: 8 reels, 2,147 meters (approximately 68 minutes 1956 release version) Not known to have been released in the United States
Note: Kozintsev disowned the release version of this film, which was reedited without his cooperation.

PIROGOV (Lenfilm, 1947)
Scenario: Yuri German
Photography: Andrei Moskvin, A. Nazarov, N. Sifrin
Production Design: Yevgeni Enei, S. Malkin
Music: Dmitri Shostakovich
Cast: Konstantin Skorobogatov, Nikolai Cherkasov, V. Chestnokov, Alexei Diki, O. Lebzak
Running time: 10 reels (80–90 minutes, exact timing not known)
Never released in the United States

BELINSKY (1953)
Scenario: Y. German, E. Serebrovskaya, G. Kozintsev
Photography: M. Magidson, Andrei Moskvin, S. Ivanov
Cast: S. Kurilov, A Borisov, V. Chestnokov, Yuri Tolubeyev
Running time not known
Never released in the United States

DON QUIXOTE (Lenfilm, 1957)
Scenario: (from the Cervantes novel) Yevgeni Schwartz
Photography: Andrei Moskvin, Apollinari Dudko, I. Gritsius, E. Rozovski
Production Design: Yevgeni Enei, V. Altman
Music: Kar-Karayev
Cast: Nicholas Cherkasov, Yuri Tolubeyev, Serafima Birman, S.

Grigorieva, Maximov
Running time: 110 minutes
New York premiere: January 20, 1961, at the 55th Street and 68th
Street Playhouse
16mm. rental and lease: Macmillan/Audio-Brandon

HAMLET (Lenfilm, 1963)
Scenario: Kozintsev (based on Boris Pasternak's translation of
Shakespeare's play)
Photography: I. Gritsius
Production Design: Yevgeni Enei, G. Kropachev, S. Virsaladze
Music: Dmitri Shostakovich
Cast: Innokenti Smoktunovski, Mikhail Nazvanov, Anastasia Ver-
tinskaya, Yuri Tolubeyev
Running time: 148 minutes
New York premiere: September 14, 1964, as the opening-night feature
at the New York Film Festival, Symphony Hall, Lincoln Center;
commercial premiere, March 15, 1966 at the Plaza Theater
16mm. rental: Macmillan: Audio/Brandon

KING LEAR (KOROL LEAR, 1971)
Scenario: Kozintsev (based on Boris Pasternak's translation of
Shakespeare)
Photography: I. Gritsius
Production Designer: Yevgeni Enei
Set Designer: Vsevolod Ulitko
Costumes: S. Virsaladze
Music: Dmitri Shostakovich
Cast: Yuri Yarvet, Elsa Radzin, Galina Volchek, Valentian Shendrikova,
Oleg Dal, K. Cebric, Lionard Merzin, Regimastas Adomaitis,
Vladimir Yemelyanov
Running time: 140 minutes
New York premiere: October 1, 1972
16mm. rental: Macmillan/Audio-Brandon

o   o   o

Note: Information about all of those films of Kozintsev's currently
available for rental in this country in 16mm. may be obtained from
Macmillan/Audio-Brandon, 34 MacQuesten Parkway South, Mount
Vernon, New York 10550. Telephone: (914) 664-5051.

Index

153